AWESOME ACTIVITIES
For BFFs

ACTIVITIES
Hours of Fun for You
and Your BEST FRIENDS!

D1341093

hinkler

PARTY GIRL
PHYSICS

  1 PARTY BUZZ

The best parties are the ones everyone talks about afterward. But that chatter wouldn't happen without **sound waves**.

WHAT'S THE SCIENCE?

Your **eardrum** picks up on **vibrations** in the air and carries them to your inner ear, which sends those messages to your brain. Funnels **amplify** sounds. The pinna (the visible outer part of the ear) acts just like a funnel, too! It further amplifies sounds as they enter the ear canal (the passage running from the outer to the middle ear).

Materials

- large piece of paper
- sticky tape
- radio
- friend

Steps

1. Roll the paper into a funnel, with a large opening at one end and a small opening at the other. Secure the paper with tape.

2. Put the small end of the funnel to your ear (but not IN your ear!). What can you hear?

3. Now stand near the radio with the funnel to your ear. Take the funnel away. Does the radio sound different?

4. Ask a friend to make some soft noises while you hold the funnel to your ear. Can you hear the very soft sounds?

DID YOU KNOW?

Sound is caused by vibrations. The bigger the vibrations, the louder the sound. Put your hand on your throat and hum. Do you feel the vibrations that are your voice?

LISTEN UP!

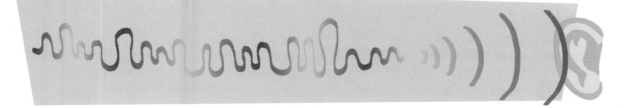

2 TURN IT UP!

Materials
- large piece of strong cardboard
- sticky tape
- friend

What's the sign of a good party? Friends, food, presents—and lots of noise, of course!

WHAT'S THE SCIENCE?

When your vocal cords vibrate, the sounds you make spread out. A funnel directs all of the sound waves toward the listener, making them louder.

Steps

1. Roll the piece of cardboard into a funnel. The opening at the small end should be about the size of your mouth.
2. Secure the cardboard with tape.
3. Ask your friend to stand at a distance. Yell something funny.
4. Put the small end of the funnel to your mouth. Shout something else. Can your friend hear you better now? Why do you think this is?

3 HEAR YOU GO!

Some of the best secrets are shared at parties. Use this experiment to find out just how much spying ears might hear …

Materials
- two friends
- drinking glass

WHAT'S THE SCIENCE?

All substances are made of **molecules**. In **denser** substances, such as solids, the molecules are very close together. **Sound energy** makes molecules vibrate, which cause the close-knit molecules to collide, meaning sound waves can easily travel through the molecules of solids.

Steps

1. Sit in a room and have your friends sit in the room next door, so you are separated by one wall.
2. Listen as your friends whisper, then talk in normal voices, and then talk loudly.
3. Now hold your glass against the wall and repeat step 2. Can you hear what they are saying more easily with or without the glass?

4 VIBRATION NATION

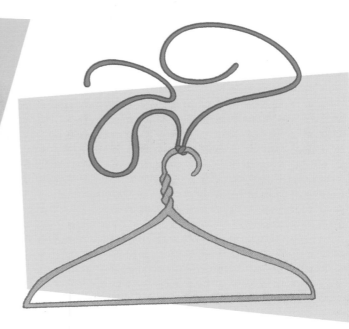

Most parents can't stand loud parties—but this will be music to their ears! Just tell them you're studying sound!

WHAT'S THE SCIENCE?

Sounds vibrate, but in the open air they tend to spread. Good sound **conductors**, such as metals, direct sounds through them.

Materials

- 2-ft (60-cm) piece of string
- coat hanger
- table
- metal objects, e.g. fork, spoon, ruler

Steps

1. Tie the string to the coat hanger, knotting the middle of the string so you are left with two strands.
2. Wrap one strand around a finger on each hand.
3. Knock the coat hanger against a table. What sound can you hear?
4. Now put your hands over your ears (not IN your ears!), while still holding both strands of string. Knock the coat hanger against the table again. What can you hear now? Try this with other metal objects in place of the coat hanger.

DID YOU KNOW?

When you put your hands over your ears, you created a path for the sound waves to travel along. This also made the sound more **resonant** than the sound you made before.

MUSICAL MATCHBOX

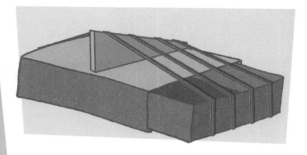

What's a party without music? (A big yawn is what it is!) A matchbox guitar should get things going!

Materials

- craft knife
- small piece of balsa wood
- empty matchbox
- 4 rubber bands

Steps

1. First, make the bridge for your guitar. Using the craft knife, cut the balsa wood into a triangular shape. The bottom edge should be a little longer than the width of the matchbox. The left edge should be straight up and down.

2. Place the triangle across the width of the matchbox with the pointed end hanging over the side. Cut off the point.

3. Lay the bridge on top of the matchbox, then open the matchbox about three-quarters of the way.

4. Put the rubber bands lengthways over the matchbox, an equal distance apart. Make sure they are tight.

5. Now raise the bridge so it lifts the rubber bands up. You're ready to make music!

WHAT'S THE SCIENCE?

Plucking rubber bands causes them to vibrate. The vibration creates sound waves, which is how guitars make noise!

DID YOU KNOW?

Brace yourself for this major party foul alert! The first guitar strings were made using the intestines of sheep. It is thought, however, that the violin has to take credit for the term "cat gut." A violin was also known as a "kit," so the strings were referred to as "kit gut." Over time, the term evolved into "cat gut." Luckily, nowadays they are made from nylon, bronze, or steel.

6 STRAW SOUNDS

Getting someone's attention at a loud party can be difficult. But not with one of these straw oboes!

WHAT'S THE SCIENCE?

Standing waves are waves that are stationary. They can vibrate back and forth on a string or in the air. Standing wave patterns are important to instruments. They hold a pattern on a vibrating string or in the air, creating a specific note, or **frequency**.

Materials

- drinking straw
- scissors

Steps

1. Squeeze one end of the straw between your fingers to flatten it.
2. Cut the tip of the straw into a long point with two diagonal snips.
3. Put the point in your mouth and blow.
4. Now cut a small hole in the straw, about halfway down. Cover the hole with your finger and blow into the straw. Then lift your finger. How does the sound change?
5. Experiment with sounds by snipping more holes in the body of the straw and covering and uncovering them while you play.

7 BOUNCE AROUND!

Have you ever been to such a great party that it felt like people were "bouncing off the walls?" They weren't, of course—but sounds were!

Materials

- drinking glass (crystal or thin-walled glasses work best)
- water

Steps

1. Run your finger around the rim of the glass. What happens?
2. Now, wet your finger with water and run it around the rim of the glass again. Keep going until something happens. Can you hear anything?
3. Put some water in the glass and repeat step 2.

WHAT'S THE SCIENCE?

Making a glass sing is a party trick even famous scientist Galileo loved. The glass vibrates because of **friction** with your finger. A clean glass and a wet finger help you to adjust the vibrations perfectly so that they resonate—creating a rich tone when the friction and the glass resonance match.

PERFECT PITCHES
8 🏠

Materials

- 5 or more identical bottles (glass is best but plastic will also work)
- water
- spoon or fork

Turn off your party playlist and make music with your friends. If possible, give each person their own bottle to play!

WHAT'S THE SCIENCE?

The air in the bottle is called an **air column**. Adding water to the bottle shortens the length of the air column, which changes the frequency of the sound caused by striking the bottles.

Steps

1. Put the bottles in a line.
2. Put a little water in the first bottle, then a bit more in the next, and so on, until you have filled all the bottles with increasing amounts of water.
3. Take the spoon or fork and strike the bottles one after the other.
4. Now strike the bottles in any order. Can you make a tune?

SCREAM TEAMS
9 🏠 ✂️

Materials

- a sound recorder on a phone, computer, tablet, or other device
- different sound "absorbers", e.g. a pillow, aluminum foil, a paper plate, a piece of foam, a raincoat

You don't always want to pump up the volume—some things need to be kept quiet. Here's how!

WHAT'S THE SCIENCE?

The vibrations you create with your voice are either **reflected** or **absorbed** by the materials around you. Soundproof materials absorb vibrations by converting their energy into tiny bits of heat, which stops the sound.

Steps

1. Place your sound recorder about 10 in (25 cm) in front of you. Speak (or scream!) into it, recording the sounds.
2. Try placing different sound absorbers in front of your mouth when you speak or yell. For safety, make sure each item is in front of your mouth, but not touching or covering it.
3. Listen to the sounds you made with each material. Which objects seem to best absorb sound?
4. Place the sound absorbers on one or both sides of your mouth to absorb parts of the vibration. Try the experiment again. Did the sound wave pattern change?

Materials

- enclosed corridor with a bare floor
- 2 blocks of wood
- enclosed carpeted area (another option is a hallway with and without a rug)

Want to find a way to cut down on the noise at your next party? Simple! Have it in a carpeted space. Carpet absorbs sound waves!

Steps

1. Stand on the bare floor.
2. Bang the blocks of wood together softly. Now bang them together loudly. What is happening?
3. Next, go to the carpeted area. Repeat step 2. What happens?

WHAT'S THE SCIENCE?

Sound bounces off flat, hard walls, but is absorbed by rugs and soundproof walls with absorbent materials such as foam.

DID YOU KNOW?

Fabric curtains, especially thick ones, can also help to reduce noise in a room!

She did it!

Lisa Randall
United States

At just 18 years old, Lisa was already winning important science talent search awards. Today, Lisa is a "particle physicist," and the first female physicist to be tenured, or given a lifelong position, at Princeton University. She is also the first tenured female theoretical physicist at MIT and Harvard University. Lisa came up with the idea that our world could be made up of much more space than we know, filled with hidden dimensions.

11 SHADOW PLAY

Materials

- dark room
- large flashlight/torch
- white or light-colored wall
- 2 friends

Want to double your guest list without having to ask permission? Turn out the lights, and party with the shadows!

WHAT'S THE SCIENCE?

Shadows occur when light cannot pass through an object. The closer an object is to the light, the larger its shadow will be.

Steps

1. Shine the flashlight/torch onto the wall.
2. Invite your friends to stand in the light. Ask one person to stand near the wall and the other to stand near the light. Whose shadow is bigger?
3. Ask them to change positions. What happens to the shadows on the wall? Whose shadow is bigger now? Why do you think this happens?

12 FRIENDLY FACES

Materials

- dark room
- chair
- friend
- large piece of stiff paper
- adhesive putty, such as Blu-Tack or Poster Putty
- bright flashlight/torch
- marker

It's always sad when the party is over. Keep your friends around even after they've gone home with these shadow drawings!

WHAT'S THE SCIENCE?

Shadows can be darker or lighter, depending on how **translucent** an object is. (In other words, how much light can seep through it.)

Steps

1. Put the chair against a wall.
2. Ask your friend to sit sideways on the chair.
3. Hang the paper on the wall behind your friend's head with some adhesive putty.
4. Set up the flashlight/torch so that it shines on your friend's head, making a shadow on the paper.
5. Using the marker, trace the outline of the shadow.

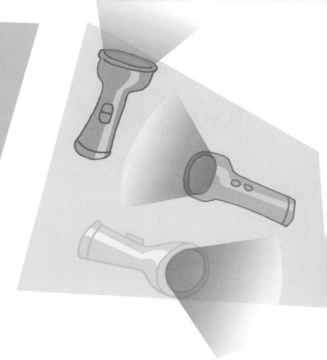

13 RAINBOW TRAILS

Shadows are cool—but rainbow shadows are MUCH cooler! This experiment is guaranteed to bring colorful fun to any slumber party.

WHAT'S THE SCIENCE?

When you mix paint, light is absorbed by the paint, so the colors get darker. But when you mix different colored lights, they combine to reflect new colors or new light frequencies. When you combine red, blue, and green light, you get white light.

Materials

- dark room
- 3 different colored lightbulbs (red, green, and blue)
- 3 flashlights/torches or lamps to put the bulbs in
- friend

Steps

1. Shine one of the colored lights around the room. Notice how different everything looks.
2. Now shine all three lights at one spot, creating overlapping circles of light. What do you see?
3. Ask your friend to hold their hand out to create a shadow where the lights overlap.
4. Try shining the different lights in different combinations. See how many different shadow colors you can create.

DID YOU KNOW?

A rainbow is made up of the colors in the **visible spectrum**, ordered from longest **wavelength** to shortest. Some people use "Roy G Biv" to help remember them:

Red
Orange
Yellow
Green
Blue
Indigo
Violet

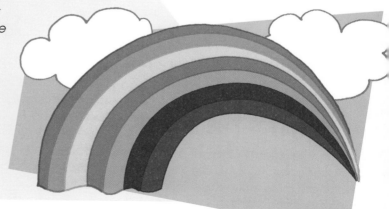

GARDEN GLORY

14

Give your party a rainbow theme—all you need is some sunlight and a hose. Your guests will love this spectacular surprise!

Materials

- garden hose

Steps

1. Turn on the hose.
2. Put your finger over the tip, creating mist.
3. Stand so the sun is behind you, and angle the hose into the air.
4. See the rainbow in the mist!

WHAT'S THE SCIENCE?

Rainbows occur when sunlight shines onto drops of water. When the rays of light hit the water droplets they are bent, or **refracted**. When the light bends it breaks up into the colors of the rainbow.

PRETTY PAIR

15

Materials

- bathroom mirror
- handheld mirror

Before your guests arrive, make sure you hit the restroom and freshen up. While you're in there, have a magical mirror moment.

Steps

1. Stand with your back to the bathroom mirror.
2. Hold the handheld mirror up to your face.
3. Count how many images of yourself you can see.
4. Now turn the handheld mirror a little. What do you notice?
5. Put your face very close to the handheld mirror. What happens?

WHAT'S THE SCIENCE?

Mirrors reflect light in straight lines. Their smooth, flat surfaces allow the light reflected off them to show accurate images. If a mirror is bent or broken, the light waves bend and the image changes—making you look stretched or cracked!

RIGHT BACK ATCHA!

Keep your guest list secret by writing everyone's names backward. With a mirror, you'll be able to read the names just fine—but nobody else will!

WHAT'S THE SCIENCE?

A mirror reflects images exactly as they bounce off it. This means we see the **mirror image** of how things normally appear.

DID YOU KNOW?

Have you ever wondered why the word "AMBULANCE" is written in reverse on the front of an ambulance? Now you know—it's so drivers can read it correctly in their rearview mirrors!

Materials

- sheets of paper
- marker pen
- small rectangular mirror

Steps

1. Write your name in large letters on a sheet of paper with the marker pen.

2. Place the mirror upright on the edge of the paper so that you can see your writing reflected. How do the letters look in the mirror? Do any of them look the same in the mirror as they do on the paper?

3. On another sheet of paper, try to write your name in reverse. Check your writing in the mirror. Does it look the right way around? Keep practicing your reverse writing.

17 RISE AND SHINE!

Surprise your friends after a sleepover with this wonderful wake-up call.

WHAT'S THE SCIENCE?

When light passes through a new material, it changes direction and refracts, breaking up into many different wavelengths. Sunlight in the air **diffracts** as it passes through water and glass.

Materials

- box about 20 in (50 cm) high
- sunny window
- clear drinking glass
- water
- large sheet of paper

Steps

1. Early on a clear, sunny morning, set up the box about 4 yds (4 m) from a window.
2. Fill the glass with water and place it on the box.
3. Look for a rainbow on the floor. Put the paper on the floor to help you see the rainbow better. What colors can you see?

18 OVER THE RAINBOW

Try this rainbow trick, then ask your friends to vote. Which did they prefer—the rainbow created by the cup or the square container?

WHAT'S THE SCIENCE?

Light passing through glass or plastic that is curved or that has sharp corners will change direction, or even reflect off of other flat surfaces. Watch as your rainbows transform.

Materials

- dark room
- flashlight/torch
- clear plastic cup
- jug of water
- friend
- clear square container

Steps

1. Switch on the flashlight/torch and point it at the ceiling. Place the cup on top of it, right way up.
2. Ask your friend to gently pour some water into the cup. Watch the ceiling for rainbows.
3. Now do the same using the square container instead of the cup. What kind of rainbows did you see this time?

19 THE RAINBOW TOUCH

So, you're dressed to the nines for your party. Now make yourself a ten with the ultimate party accessory—a rainbow on your hand!

WHAT'S THE SCIENCE?

Light usually travels in straight lines. In this case, the water changes the direction of light because water is denser, but still transparent. We see rainbows when the light frequencies of white light are spread out through this diffraction.

DID YOU KNOW?

Rainbows appear when sunlight passes through water in the air at just the right angle. Too high or too low, and the rainbow won't show. Rainbows appear in different places if you change YOUR angle, too!

Materials

- water
- frying pan or skillet
- small mirror
- strong sunlight

Steps

1. Pour the water into the pan and place the pan in sunlight.

2. Place the mirror against the side of the pan.

3. Place your hand in front of the mirror. Where is the rainbow reflected? What is creating the prism (a transparent object that reflects light) for the light to travel through?

20 CELLOPHANE SENSATIONS

Poll your party guests for their favorite colors. Then make a wall tribute showing all of their favorites!

WHAT'S THE SCIENCE?

Red, blue, and green are called the primary colors of light. When two primary colors are combined, they create secondary colors—magenta, yellow, and cyan. If you combine all three colors and shine your flashlight onto them, you will see a pure or off-white color—called "white light."

Materials

- flashlight/torch
- white wall
- red, blue, and green cellophane

Steps

1. Shine the flashlight/torch onto a white wall.
2. Cover the flashlight with red and green cellophane. What color is made on the wall?
3. Now use red and blue cellophane. What color appears?
4. Then try blue and green cellophane. What color does this make?
5. What other colors can you make using the cellophane? Can you make black?

21 WHITE LIGHT WONDER

Take your party to the next color dimension by mixing up some magenta (blue overlaps red) and cyan (green overlaps blue)—two new, surefire color faves!

WHAT'S THE SCIENCE?

The primary colors of light (red, green, and blue) can be combined to make the main colors used in mixing dyes—cyan, magenta, and yellow.

Materials

- 3 flashlights/torches
- red, blue, and green cellophane
- sticky tape
- white wall

Steps

1. Cover the light of each flashlight/torch with a different color of cellophane, then turn them on.
2. Place the flashlights about 4 in (10 cm) apart on a table and shine them at a white wall.
3. Make sure that the light from each flashlight overlaps with the others. What can you see on the wall?

22 SUPER SPINNER

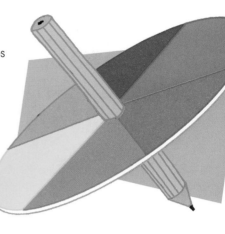

Materials

- pair of compasses
- piece of white cardboard
- scissors
- protractor
- colored pencils
- pencil

Have each of your guests make one of these beautiful and surprising toys. They can take them home as party souvenirs!

WHAT'S THE SCIENCE?

White light is made up of all the colors of the rainbow.

Steps

1. Using the pair of compasses, draw a circle on the cardboard and cut it out.
2. Use the protractor to mark out six equal sections.
3. Color each section with the following colors: red, blue, green, yellow, orange, and violet.
4. Push the pencil through the center of the circle so that you can spin it like a top. What happens to the colors when you spin it?

---

23 SILVER SPOON

A good party is filled with laughter. Get ready for some big laughs when you see yourself reflected in your spoon!

WHAT'S THE SCIENCE?

When an image is reflected on a **concave** or **convex** surface, the image becomes **distorted**. This is because concave mirrors bend reflected light inward, and convex mirrors bend light outward.

Materials

- shiny spoon

Steps

1. Hold the spoon up to your face with the back of the spoon pointing toward you.
2. Move the spoon away from your face. How does your reflection change? Is that what you expected?
3. Turn the spoon around. What do you see now?

⭐ SCATTERED

LIGHT

Each guest can make their own kaleidoscope, using lots of small colorful objects.

WHAT'S THE SCIENCE?

Different **geometric** patterns form when light bounces and reflects off objects and mirrors.

DID YOU KNOW?

The world's largest kaleidoscope is in Mount Tremper, New York. It stands 64 ft (19.5 m) tall. There is no eyepiece—visitors stand (or lie down!) inside the kaleidoscope and look up to watch the magic happen.

Materials

- 8 x 4 in (20 x 10 cm) rectangle of clear cellophane
- markers
- clear tape
- cardboard tube, cut to 8 in (20 cm) long
- 4 in (10 cm) square of black construction paper
- pencil
- 4 in (10 cm) square of plastic wrap
- beads, confetti, and sequins
- 4 in (10 cm) square of waxed paper
- rubber band
- colorful tissue and stickers

Steps

1. Lay the clear cellophane rectangle so the long edges are at the top and bottom. Draw two dotted lines along the rectangle, dividing it into thirds.

2. Fold the rectangle along the dotted lines, forming a 3D triangle.

3. Secure the triangle with tape.

4. Slide the triangle into the cardboard tube.

5. Stand the tube on the black construction paper. Trace a circle around the end.

6. Using the pencil, poke a hole in the center of the construction paper and then tape the paper onto the end of the tube.

7. Place the plastic wrap over the other end of the tube, pressing it into the tube to create a "sack."

8. Fill the "sack" with small, colorful items such as beads, confetti, and sequins.

9. Top the sack with the waxed paper. Secure the paper and plastic wrap with the rubber band, then trim the edges.

10. Using markers, colorful tissue, and stickers, decorate the outside of your kaleidoscope.

11. Look through the tube with one eye. Slowly turn your new kaleidoscope—and enjoy the sights!

COLOR CODES

There's nothing like bonding over shared secrets at a party. Use these decoders to reveal hidden secrets for everyone to enjoy!

WHAT'S THE SCIENCE?

Red light is part of sunlight. When ink that is NOT red is seen through a red filter, it appears darker and stands out—while the red light blends into the red writing. The red cellophane blocks or reflects the red light, making the blue reflection from your marker easy to read.

Materials

- thick cardboard sheet
- scissors
- red cellophane
- pale blue marker
- cup of water
- blank piece of paper

Steps

1. Cut rectangles about 1 x 2 in (2.5 x 5 cm) from the cardboard sheet. Cut a section out of the center of each rectangle, to form "frames."

2. Stick the frames to the red cellophane. Cut away any excess cellophane.

3. Dip the pale blue marker in water so it will write faintly.

4. Using the weak marker, write secret messages to your friends on the paper.

5. Use the cellophane decoders to read each other's secret messages!

DID YOU KNOW?

"Cryptography" means "secret" + "writing" in Greek. Some secret messages use light blue writing with red hash marks on top. The red cellophane "erases" the red hash marks, making the blue message clear.

MAGIC MAGNIFIER

Show your guests how to turn their little secrets into big messages—just add water!

Materials

- sheets of paper
- friends
- pens
- scissors
- piece of cardboard
- plastic wrap
- clear tape
- eyedropper
- container of water

WHAT'S THE SCIENCE?

Water can act like a convex lens, making an image look bigger by bending light rays outward as they pass through it.

Steps

1. Have your friends write secret messages in tiny letters on the sheets of paper.
2. Cut a hole about 1 in (2.5 cm) wide in the cardboard.
3. Stretch the plastic wrap over the hole and tape it in place.
4. Using the eyedropper, squeeze a drop of water onto the plastic wrap.
5. Hold the cardboard "magnifying glass" over the secret notes.
6. Look through the water drop. Can you read the messages?
7. Move the cardboard closer and farther away from the paper. Can you still read the notes?

FUNNY FOIL

Make your guests disappear using nothing but aluminum foil. One minute you see them—the next you don't!

Materials

- roll of aluminum foil
- scissors

Steps

1. Cut a 10-in (25-cm) length of foil. Be careful to keep it smooth.
2. Look at your reflection in the shiny side of the foil. It won't be perfect, but you should be able to see yourself clearly.
3. Scrunch up the foil and then spread it out again.
4. Look for your reflection. Where has it gone?

WHAT'S THE SCIENCE?

When an object's surface is smooth, it reflects light. When the object is scrunched, the reflection will "disappear!" This happens because the light is scattered in all directions.

BREAKING THE RULES

Materials

- deep glass bowl or clear plastic container
- water
- ruler

This is one wild party trick that won't even get you in trouble. (Phew!)

WHAT'S THE SCIENCE?

Objects look different in water because light refracts as it passes through the water.

Steps

1. Fill up the bowl with water.
2. Lower the ruler into the bowl of water. Only put it in halfway. How does the ruler look now?
3. Slowly pull the ruler out. Has it changed?
4. Put the ruler back into the bowl and observe again.

SUPER SHIELD

Materials

- large plastic container
- water
- tissue paper
- drinking glass

Every party needs snacks. While you're in the kitchen, grab a glass and a piece of paper and see how water + air = magic!

WHAT'S THE SCIENCE?

Air takes up space, or has **volume**, even though we can't see it with our eyes. This is a basic **property of matter**! Air bubbles are pockets of air that float to the water's surface because they are less dense—unless they are trapped, like the air in the glass in this experiment.

Steps

1. Pour the water into the plastic container until it's about three-quarters full.
2. Crumple the tissue paper into a ball. Wedge it into the bottom of the glass.
3. Carefully flip the glass upside down and lower it into the plastic container, keeping it straight.
4. Watch what happens. Does any water "sneak" into the cup? Is the paper getting wet?
5. Remove the glass from the water, then remove the paper from the glass. Is the paper wet?

30 TOPPLE THE TILES

Ever noticed how the energy builds (and so does the volume!) as people arrive at a party? The same thing can happen when one object collides with another. Grab some dominoes and watch energy transfer occur for yourself!

WHAT'S THE SCIENCE?

All objects have both **potential energy** and **kinetic energy**. Dominoes are a perfect example. When they are standing still, they have potential energy. But once the first domino is tapped, you add a **force**, changing potential energy to kinetic energy. When that domino hits the next one, the kinetic energy is transferred—and the chain reaction begins!

Materials

- 2 packs of dominoes
- large flat area, e.g. table

Steps

1. Line the dominoes up on their ends along the table, about 3/4 in (2 cm) apart.
2. Tap the first domino and watch what happens.

DID YOU KNOW?

What you just watched is called a "domino effect," where one action causes a chain of events. Another domino effect occurs during storms when trees fall. What other domino effects can you think of?

31 CRAZY CUP

What do playing with decorations and jumping around have in common? Both are essential ingredients for a perfect party!

WHAT'S THE SCIENCE?

In science, opposites **attract**! Positive **charges** move toward **negative charges** in physics. However, when two alike charges are near each other, they **repel** one another

Materials

- hundreds and thousands cake decorations or round colored sprinkles
- small plastic container with a lid
- woolen cloth/sweater

Steps

1. Place the hundreds and thousands in the plastic container and put the lid on.
2. Rub the lid with the cloth to charge it.
3. Carefully run your finger across the top of the lid.
4. Do the hundreds and thousands stay up or fall down? Why do you think this is?

She did it!

Amanda Barnard
Australia

"Hundreds and thousands" look pretty tiny, don't they? But they're enormous compared to the things studied by Australian research scientist Amanda Barnard. Growing up, Amanda had no idea what she wanted to do or who she wanted to be. But when she heard about nanotechnology she became excited. Nanotech scientists move **atoms** and molecules to conceive incredible new devices. They measure objects in nanometers: one nanometer is equal to only one billionth of a meter! In fact, the objects they work with are so miniscule that scientists have to rely on special microscopic equipment to see them. Today Amanda uses computer models to show how objects can be made faster, cheaper, and better.

32 PUFF POPS

Materials
- bowl
- puffed cereal
- plastic spoon
- woolen cloth/sweater

What comes to mind when you hear the word "pop?" Balloons? Music? Well, now you can add puffed cereal to the list!

WHAT'S THE SCIENCE?

Rubbing the spoon gives it a negative charge, which attracts the cereal. However, when the cereal touches the spoon it becomes negatively charged, too. The two objects then repel one another.

Steps
1. Fill the bowl with puffed cereal.
2. Rub the spoon with the cloth.
3. Hold the spoon close to the cereal bowl. Watch what the cereal does when the spoon gets near it.
4. What happens next? Does the cereal stay near the spoon?

---

33 PEAS TEASE

Materials
- drinking glass
- dried peas
- water
- metal lid

Want to see some dancing at your party? Just add water and watch these peas move!

WHAT'S THE SCIENCE?

Osmosis happens when water passes through the membrane, or exterior, of a living thing. Peas, just like all living organisms, are made of cells with semi-permeable membranes, which means they allow water to pass through and enter them.

Steps
1. Fill the glass to the brim with dried peas.
2. Add water, again filling the glass to the brim.
3. Place the glass on top of the metal lid.
4. Watch how the peas move.

DID YOU KNOW?

Osmosis can be used to remove an egg's shell without breaking it! All you have to do is soak the egg in vinegar.

SUPER SPOON

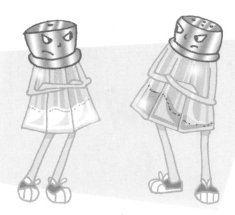

Take charge of your snack table! Grab some condiments and spoon feed everyone a little bit of magic.

WHAT'S THE SCIENCE?

Salt is made up of two charged elements. Sodium (NA+) is positive and Chloride (Cl-) is negative. The pepper is positively charged compared to the salt, so it is attracted to the spoon first.

Materials

- plastic spoon
- woolen cloth/ sweater
- salt
- pepper

Steps

1. Rub the spoon with the cloth.
2. Mix the salt and pepper together.
3. Hold the spoon above the salt and pepper and slowly lower it until the pepper "jumps up" and clings to it.

IT'S ELECTRIC!

Materials

- balloon
- hole punch
- paper

Look around your party at your friends. Are any of your friends really different from you? Opposites attract, right? It's the same in science!

WHAT'S THE SCIENCE?

When the balloon is rubbed on your head, negative **electrons** from your hair are transferred onto the balloon. The paper has a positive charge. Negative and positive charges are attracted to one another, so the paper sticks to the balloon. The act of them coming together is called ion **propulsion**.

Steps

1. Blow up the balloon just enough so it will fit in your hand. Tie it.
2. Using the hole punch, cut a small circle in the paper.
3. Rub the balloon on your hair about 15 times. Don't press too hard, and make sure that your hair is clean first.
4. Now hold the balloon close to the paper and see what happens.

IT TAKES TWO

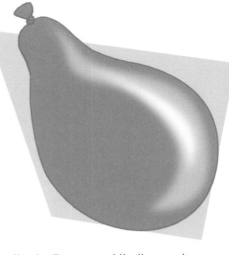

Materials

- balloons
- string
- woolen cloth/sweater
- thick paper

Try this trick at a party during winter. One of your guests is bound to be wearing a woolen sweater. Before you know it, the party will be electric!

Steps

1. Blow up the balloons and tie the ends.
2. Attach string to the end of each balloon.
3. Rub the balloons against the woolen cloth.
4. Hold them up by the string. What happens?
5. Place the paper between the balloons. What happens?

WHAT'S THE SCIENCE?

Static electricity occurs when an object has more negative or positive charges on its surface and needs to **neutralize** the charge, creating **electrostatic discharges**—or sparks.

HOLY HAIR!

Who needs tape? You can decorate your walls with balloons using just your hair!

WHAT'S THE SCIENCE?

Rubbing one substance against another substance causes a buildup of electrons. The wall is neutral until it comes into contact with a charged substance, such as a charged balloon. Its electrons are repelled by the negatively charged balloon, making it positively charged—and causing the balloon to stick!

Materials

- inflated balloon
- blank wall

Steps

1. Rub the balloon against your hair.
2. Hold the balloon up against the wall. What happens?

CRAZY COMB

After a good boogie, it's time to fix that messy hair! Grab a comb and collect yourself—and some electrons!

WHAT'S THE SCIENCE?

The atoms in your hair have more electrons, which are negatively charged, than **protons**, which are positively charged. Electrons build up in the hair when it is combed, due to friction. The electrons transfer to the comb, then draw the positive charge in the water nearer—causing an attraction.

DID YOU KNOW?

Forensic scientists sometimes examine combs to solve mysteries! Hair samples, which contain DNA, often serve as useful evidence when determining if a person was at a crime scene.

Materials

- sink with faucet/tap
- clean, dry hair
- plastic comb

Steps

1. Turn on the faucet/tap to release a thin stream of water.
2. Run the comb through your hair 15 times.
3. Hold the comb near the water stream but not touching it. What does the water do?

TWINKLING TIARA

Use optical fibers from an old toy to make this new, reusable party accessory, and shine on through the night!

WHAT'S THE SCIENCE?

Fiber optic cables are made of a pure glass that directs light through a tube, like a straw. The cables are extremely thin and flexible.

Materials

- fiber optic wand
- basic headband
- electrical tape the same color as the headband, or a complementary color
- decorations, such as fake flowers, fake jewels, or geometric shapes
- glue gun or other glue for decorations

Steps

1. If needed, take the casing off of your wand. You may need to ask an adult for help.
2. Attach the wand's ON/OFF switch to one side of your headband with electrical tape. Make sure the switch is slightly above your ear and on the outside edge of the headband.
3. Decorate your headband to look like a crown or tiara. Arrange the optical fibers on the headband so that they light up your design.
4. Turn it on!

DID YOU KNOW?

The telephone cables you see along the highway are mostly made from fiber optics—not from copper wire, as many people think.

40 WHERE'S THE PARTY?

Materials

- needle
- magnet
- string
- small piece of card
- pencil
- jar
- compass

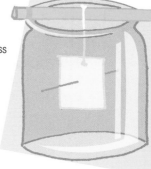

It's one thing to be fashionably late to a party, but you don't want to miss all the fun! This compass will keep you from getting lost.

WHAT'S THE SCIENCE?

A compass's needle acts as a magnet and lines up with the **Earth's magnetic field**.

Steps

1. Rub the needle in one direction against the magnet to magnetize it.
2. Tie one end of the string to the card and the other to the pencil. Push the needle into the card until it sticks through the center.
3. Lay the pencil across the top of the jar so the card hangs inside but doesn't touch the bottom. The needle should be able to spin freely.
4. Check the compass. The needle and compass should point in the same direction. Don't bring the needle too close to the compass, and keep the magnet away from both.

41 MAGNET MANIA

Materials

- any items from around your house, such as forks, spoons, paper clips, aluminum foil, pencils, soft toys
- magnet

Divide your guests into two teams and see how many magnetic objects each team can find!

WHAT'S THE SCIENCE?

Objects with stronger magnetism have more of their molecules' electrons spinning and rotating in the same way—because they are part of a solid crystal pattern. When groups of molecules, or grains, are lined up in the same north-south direction, it makes a metal strongly magnetic.

Steps

1. Organize your items into those that you think are magnetic and those that are not.
2. Test the items. If the magnet attaches to the item, it is magnetic.
3. Make a list of the items that are magnetic.

42 CLIP CLIQUE

Get all your friends to help build this magical magnetic friendship chain!

Materials

- friends
- paper clips
- strong magnet

Steps

1. Give each guest a paper clip.
2. Take a strong magnet and hold your paper clip up to it.
3. Ask one of your friends to hold her paper clip to yours, keeping your paper clip attached to the magnet.
4. Keep going, having each person add their paper clip to the chain.
5. Separate the first paper clip from the magnet. What happens to the other paper clips?

WHAT'S THE SCIENCE?

Magnetic induction occurs when a weak magnetic metal touches a strong magnet. A strong magnet's magnetic units line up in a north–south direction, like neat hair. A weak magnet is like messy hair; its units are jumbled. If you place a weak magnet (like a paper clip) near a strong magnet, the strong magnet lines up the units in the weak one, making it more magnetic.

43 DANCING DOLLS

Worn out from dancing? Let these mini-me dolls boogie down in your place while you sit back and enjoy the show!

Materials

- 4 bricks
- thin sheet of plastic
- friends
- sheets of paper
- colored pencils or markers
- scissors
- dry tissue or crumpled paper

Steps

1. Stand the four bricks up on their longest sides.
2. Place the plastic sheet on top of the bricks.
3. Ask each of your friends to draw a picture of themselves on the paper and cut it out.
4. Place the dolls under the plastic sheet.
5. Rub the plastic quickly with the dry tissue or crumpled paper. What happens to the "dolls?"

WHAT'S THE SCIENCE?

Static electricity causes negatively and positively charged objects to move toward one another. If the dolls had the same charges, they would actually "dance" away from one another.

44 HOW CHARMING!

Materials

- lamp
- piece of paper
- scissors
- string
- clear tape

Want to make your party a bit more exotic? Try adding some belly dancing—or maybe even a spinning snake show!

WHAT'S THE SCIENCE?

As air gets hot, the molecules begin to move more rapidly, bouncing away from each other. The air expands, becomes lighter, and rises upward. This movement is how wind is formed. As air is heated by a light bulb, it rises upward, turning the spiral.

Steps

1. Turn the lamp on, so the bulb can warm up.
2. Cut the piece of paper into the shape of a spiral snake.
3. Cut a piece of string and tape it to the end of the snake's tail.
4. Hold the snake over the lamp without letting it touch the bulb.
5. Watch how the snake responds to the lamp's heat.

45 FOOD FUN

No party is complete without a final kitchen raid. While you're there, grab some of these items and see which ones float!

Materials

- bucket
- water
- apple
- carrot
- potato
- orange

WHAT'S THE SCIENCE?

Buoyancy is the force that a fluid puts on an object that is submerged in it. When something floats, the weight of the water that the object displaces is equal to the buoyancy pushing against it. Lighter and airier objects are less dense, so they are buoyant. Objects with less air are denser, so they sink.

Steps

1. Fill the bucket with water.
2. Put all the fruit and vegetables in the water. What happens? Are they all floating?

46 STRING SWINGS

We know you and your friends can dance, but did you know that paper clips can, too?

WHAT'S THE SCIENCE?

Energy from one item can give several others a "push"—without even touching! The energy from the swinging spoon is transferred from the string with the spoon to the strings with paper clips. Depending on the length of the paper clip string and its distance from the spoon string, it will swing at a different rate.

Materials

- string
- scissors
- ruler
- friends
- spoon
- metal paper clips
- rope

Steps

1. Cut two pieces of string, each 12 in (30 cm) long.
2. Cut a piece for each of your friends, but make these pieces shorter than the first two.
3. Tie the spoon to one of the long pieces of string and a paper clip to the other.
4. Tie a paper clip to each of the shorter pieces of string.
5. Tie all of the pieces of string to the rope, spreading them out so there is at least 1 in (2.5 cm) between each piece.
6. Hang the rope so that it is taut, or tight.
7. Swing the spoon. What happens?

47 THINK TW-ICE!

When the party is wrapping up and everyone's worn out, it's time to chill!

WHAT'S THE SCIENCE?

Warm air heats the surface of an ice cube. If you keep the air around the ice cube cold, it won't melt as quickly. Insulators that trap heat or keep heat out can help to maintain the temperature of an object.

Materials

- friends
- bowl
- ice cubes
- "insulator materials," such as felt, foil, newspaper, plastic wrap, etc., each cut into 5 in (13 cm) squares
- timer

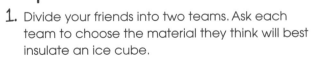

Steps

1. Divide your friends into two teams. Ask each team to choose the material they think will best insulate an ice cube.
2. Have each team wrap an ice cube in the material they have selected. Set the timer for 10 minutes.
3. Unwrap the ice cubes and see which one has melted the least.
4. Repeat the experiment using different insulators.

WONDER WORDS

absorbed—Energy is absorbed when a substance takes up some of the energy from another medium, such as light being absorbed as heat in Earth's surface.

air column—The air in an object such as a musical instrument, which is made to vibrate by blowing into or striking it. The pitch produced relates to the length of the air column, which can be changed by covering holes or sliding parts of the instrument. Can also refer to a segment of the atmosphere, often measured from Earth to the edge of outer space.

amplify—To increase the loudness of a sound by increasing the height of a sound wave and increasing the energy in the wave.

atoms—The building blocks of all matter. An atom is the smallest particle of a substance that still has the properties of that substance. The various types of atoms are called elements. An atom of gold, for example, is the smallest particle of that element possible.

attract—To pull forward or together by force. Opposite charges, for example, attract each other.

buoyancy—An object's ability to float or rise in liquid or air.

concave—Concave surfaces bow inwards.

conductor—A substance or material that conducts (channels or transmits) heat, electricity or sound.

convex—Convex surfaces bow outwards. A convex lens bows out on both sides.

dense—Tightly packed with molecules.

diffracts—When light changes direction and intensity as it is reflected off of surfaces.

distorted—Changed from its natural condition, proportion, or shape.

eardrum—A thin membrane on the edge of the middle ear that vibrates when sound waves come in contact with it.

Earth's magnetic field—The magnetic field that is created by the movement of the magnetic iron in Earth's core. It extends outwards from Earth and meets up with solar winds.

electrons—The smallest of the three particles that make up atoms (sub-atomic particles). These carry a negative charge and surround the nucleus of an atom.

electrostatic discharge—The sparks caused when static electricity is neutralized.

force—An influence that affects a change in another object.

frequency—A measure of how often a wave "vibrates" in a given amount of time. For example, light waves travel in Hz, or waves per second.

friction—Resistance caused by one object rubbing against another.

geometric—Describes anything relating to geometry, which is the mathematical study of shapes, the positions of objects related to each other.

kinetic energy—Energy that an object has due to its motion.

magnetic induction—Describes how an electric current is created when it runs across a conductor, such as iron, passing through a magnetic field.

mirror image—The image of an object as it would appear in a mirror.

molecules—Molecules are several atoms bonded together.

negative charges—The electrical charge an object has when it has more electrons than protons.

neutralize—Making positive and negative charges equal.

positive charges—The electrical charge an object has when it has more protons than electrons.

potential energy—Energy that an object has that is stored and ready for use.

property of matter—The characteristics that can be used to describe all matter. For example, all matter has weight and volume. Matter can be solid, liquid, or gas. There are many properties that scientists observe.

propulsion—Moving an object directly with the use of a force.

protons—Located in the nucleus (the center of an atom), protons are sub-atomic particles that determine an element's "type." Protons have a positive charge, and they share the nucleus with neutrons, which have a neutral charge.

reflected—The bouncing back of light, heat, or sound waves from a surface.

refracted—When light is bent as it passes from one medium to another.

repel—To push back or away by force. Matching charges, for example, repel each other.

resonant—Describes the process in which an object increases the intensity or amplification of a sound in response to another object or force having the same frequency. Everything has a natural frequency, which is the frequency at which it will vibrate or make a sound. Resonant frequencies occur when the frequency of a force matches the natural frequency of the object.

Sound energy— The energy produced by sound vibrations as they travel through a material. Sound cannot travel in a vacuum.

Sound waves—Sound waves are what our ears detect when matter vibrates. If a bell is struck, for example, it vibrates the air around it, and that vibrating air reaches our ear column. Our brains interpret this as sound. Sound is measured by determining how much energy is traveling in vibrating matter.

static electricity—Static electricity is a charge that builds up on the surface of an object.

translucent—A substance that lets only some light pass through it, such as a lens in a pair of sunglasses.

vibrations—Repeated, regular movements caused when a particle of matter (such as an atom) or energy (such as light) moves. Vibrations repeat over and over, fast or slow.

visible spectrum—The range of colors produced when light is separated by a prism. These colors are represented by the rainbow.

volume—The amount of 3-dimensional space than an object or substance occupies, or takes up.

wavelength—The distance between two identical points in two consecutive waves, such as the distance between two crests. The wavelength helps measure how much energy a wave of light or sound carries.

ROCK STAR
EARTH SCIENCES

48 ★ HAVING A BALL

Who knew it could be this easy to make an incredible model of Earth? Soon you'll have the world at your fingertips!

WHAT'S THE SCIENCE?

Earth is made up of three layers: the **core, mantle** and **crust**. It can be 11 730° F (6500° C) inside Earth—hot enough to melt metal and rock! The core is made up of two layers. The inner core is solid metal, and the outer core is liquid metal. The mantle is made up of both solid and liquid (molten) rock (which is called **magma**), and the crust is made of solid rock.

Materials

- large styrofoam ball
- set of colored markers or paints
- world map (for reference)
- knife (and an adult to help with it!)
- heavy gauge craft wire
- fishing line

Steps

1. On the outside of the styrofoam ball, draw and color in Earth's continents and oceans. Don't forget to also include the **north pole** and **south pole**. Add in some mountains and rivers. Don't forget to include your capital city!

2. Cut the styrofoam ball in half across the middle, from top to bottom—have an adult help you do this. Now, on the inside of the ball, draw in Earth's layers.

3. Earth's core is the hot spot in the center of the planet. Use a red marker or paint to color Earth's core in the center of the ball.

4. Earth's mantle is the area between the core and the crust. Color Earth's mantle in brown or orange.

5. Paint a thin black or dark brown line around the edge of the circle to represent Earth's crust.

6. Bend two pieces of craft wire in half and twist the ends a few times to create two loops. Insert the wire loops in the "tops" of each half of Earth. Thread the fishing line through both wire loops and hang your planet so the two halves sit together, but you can look inside and see the insides of Earth!

DID YOU KNOW?

*The core (both the inner and outer layers) is made of **nickel** and **iron**. These are **magnetic** metals that give Earth its magnetic field.*

EDIBLE EARTH

49

Ever felt so hungry you thought you could eat the whole world? Well now you can!

WHAT'S THE SCIENCE?

Earth's crust is very thin—just 3–6 mi (5–10 km) thick under the oceans, and 22–44 mi (35–70 km) under the continents. The mantle, on the other hand, is 1800 mi (2900 km) thick!

Materials

- 1 gumdrop (also known as a wine gum, jujube or jube)
- 14 marshmallows
- 1 tablespoon butter
- large, microwave-safe bowl
- 2 cups crispy rice cereal
- chocolate sauce that hardens
- knife (and an adult to help with it!)

Steps

1. Press the gumdrop into the center of a marshmallow.
2. Put the butter and remaining marshmallows into the bowl. Microwave on high for one minute (ask an adult to help you). Careful—the marshmallows will puff up and will be very hot!
3. Stir in the cereal. Allow the mixture to cool.
4. With wet hands, roll the mixture into a ball. Press the first marshmallow into the center and shape the ball around it, covering it entirely.
5. Chill the ball in the freezer for 30 minutes.
6. Remove the ball from the freezer and cover it completely with chocolate sauce. Wait for the sauce to harden.
7. Now cut your Earth in half. Check out the layers!

EXPLORE THE CORE

50

Who knew apples were so much like the Earth?

WHAT'S THE SCIENCE?

The thin skin on an apple is a great example of just how thin Earth's crust is compared to the mantle. In fact, Earth's crust is even thinner than it looks on the apple stamp!

Materials

- apple, cut in half from top to bottom
- ink pad
- large sheet of paper
- pen

Steps

1. Press one half of the apple onto the ink pad.
2. Press the apple against the paper for a few seconds, applying a little pressure.
3. Carefully lift the apple off the paper. You should now have an ink stamp of the apple.
4. Notice any similarities between your stamp and Earth's interior? Label your stamp. Write where you think Earth's crust would be, and label the core and the mantle.

51 CRACKING UP

Feeling a little unsteady? It could be the Earth moving under your feet!

WHAT'S THE SCIENCE?

Earth's crust is made up of **tectonic plates**. The plates are constantly sliding around on top of the mantle. When the plates bump into each other or slide against each other, this changes the surface of Earth.

Materials

- graham crackers/ digestive biscuits
- wax paper

Steps

1. Put two crackers/biscuits side by side on the wax paper. The space between them is like a rift, or crack in the ocean floor. Slowly push them apart. As Earth's plates move apart, new ocean floors and underwater mountain ranges are created by magma oozing out of Earth's mantle.

2. Now move the crackers toward one another. Do they crumble when they meet? Many mountain ranges on Earth were formed when plates "crumbled" together.

3. Now move two crackers toward one another and slide one beneath the other. If this were happening with Earth's plates, the bottom plate would melt from heat and pressure before becoming magma.

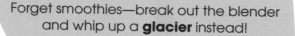

52 QUICK AND FREEZY

Forget smoothies—break out the blender and whip up a **glacier** instead!

WHAT'S THE SCIENCE?

Glaciers form when snow that falls in winter doesn't completely melt in summer. It accumulates in sheets, creating giant "rivers of ice", which flow across the landscape, carving the stone below. Glaciers are melting more quickly today than they were a century ago. Many scientists believe this is because of **global warming**.

Materials

- blender
- ice cubes
- tray
- rubber gloves
- freezer

Steps

1. Blend the ice cubes (ask an adult for help), then tip the blended ice onto the tray.

2. Put on your rubber gloves and pack the ice into a ball.

3. Let it melt for a minute, then place the ice ball in the freezer.

4. Take out your ice ball. Is it a big clump of ice?

53 POLAR PLAY

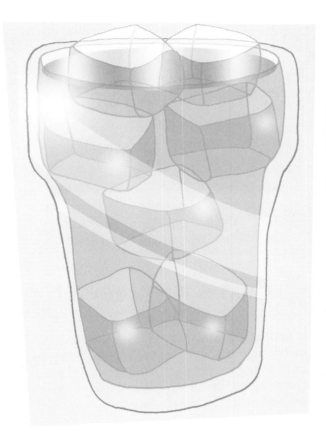

Go ahead—make a little mess! It's all in the name of science!

WHAT'S THE SCIENCE?

Polar ice caps are large sheets of ice located at the Earth's poles. It is thought the polar ice caps are shrinking due to global warming. Melting polar ice caps are changing ocean conditions, causing the destruction of marine plant and animal habitats and creating rising sea levels.

Materials

- ice cubes
- large cup
- enough water to fill the cup

Steps

1. Half-fill the cup with ice cubes. The ice in this experiment represents the polar ice caps.

2. Fill the cup with water. Try to get the water level as close to the top as possible without overfilling the cup. The water represents Earth's oceans.

3. Now, wait for the polar ice caps (the ice cubes) to melt. What do you think will happen?

DID YOU KNOW?

Due to the tilted axis of the Earth, polar ice caps get sunlight on an angle and have long winters with little sun, resulting in lower surface temperatures. Throughout the ages, polar ice caps have varied in size and growth according to the climate. During the ice ages, polar ice caps covered more of Earth than they do now.

54 POP ROCKS

Share this experiment with your science teacher, and maybe you'll be allowed to chew gum in school after all!

WHAT'S THE SCIENCE?

Rocks change from one kind to another through a process called the **rock cycle**. The rock cycle begins when magma cools and hardens to form **igneous rock**. Igneous rock breaks down into **sediments**, which collect and harden over thousands of years, forming **sedimentary rock**. If you look at a cliff and can see different layers, it is sedimentary rock. Over time, sedimentary rock is buried in Earth's crust, where heat and pressure transform it into **metamorphic rock**.

Materials

- chewing gum
- small plate
- packet of Pop Rocks

Steps

1. Put a piece of chewing gum on the plate. Pretend it is a piece of sedimentary rock. Now put it in your mouth.

2. Chew on the gum. The heat in your mouth and the pressure of your teeth will change its form.

3. Remove the gum from your mouth and fold some Pop Rocks into it. Chew it again— this will increase the heat and pressure. Your piece of gum has now been transformed into metamorphic rock.

4. Remove the gum from your mouth and place it on the plate. Allow it to cool and harden. Now the gum represents igneous rock.

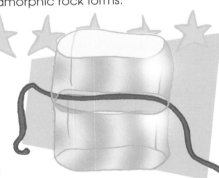

55 ROCKIN' PANCAKES

It's breakfast time—who's up for some sedimentary rock and syrup?

Materials

- sultanas, coconut, and nuts (Be careful to check if anyone is allergic to nuts before starting the experiment!)
- pancake mix (ready-made)
- frying pan
- stove
- spatula

Steps

1. Add sultanas, coconut, and nuts to your pancake mix. This is similar to sedimentary rock.
2. Now, with an adult, cook your pancake. As it is cooking, press down on the pancake with a spatula to flatten it. Has the pancake hardened and changed shape? This is similar to the way metamorphic rock forms.

WHAT'S THE SCIENCE?

Metamorphic rock forms when sedimentary or igneous rocks are changed due to great heat or pressure or from exposure to hot, **mineral** fluids. Due to this heat and pressure, metamorphic rocks look like many fine layers or "sheets" that are densely packed together.

56 YOU ROCK!

It can get super hot inside Earth—but these rocks will cool you down!

Materials

- two ice cubes
- piece of thin string or thread
- paper towel or cloth

Steps

1. Place one ice cube on a flat surface.
2. Lay the string across the ice cube, with the ends hanging over the sides.
3. Place the second ice cube on top of the string. Using the paper towel, push down on the ice cubes so that they are pressed together. Hold the pressure for a minute, then gently let go.
4. After 10 seconds, pick up the ice by the string. The ice cubes melted under the pressure, and then re-froze together!

WHAT'S THE SCIENCE?

Heat and pressure both cause solids to melt. However, during the process of metamorphism (meaning 'change in form'), rocks don't melt. They are transformed into denser, more compact rocks. Mineral components rearrange or **react** with fluid entering the rocks to create new minerals. A metamorphic rock can change into another type of rock if it undergoes further changes in pressure and temperature.

57 BLOW 'N' GO

Materials
- loose soil
- tray
- hair dryer (you may need an extension cord)

Stop frying your poor hair—use your hair dryer on the soil instead, and see what happens!

WHAT'S THE SCIENCE?

Soil can be affected by the weather. It can be worn away by wind and rain. This is known as soil **erosion**. Sand dunes are a spectacular form of wind erosion. Dunes are mounds of mostly clean sand, which move with the wind. Dunes have been known to bury oases—and even entire ancient cities!

Steps
1. Lay the soil loosely in the tray. (Do this outside—it will get messy!)
2. Tilt the hair dryer on its side and blow air across the soil. What happens? Is some of the soil being blown away?

---

58 MAGNET MANIA

Materials
- rocks (find as many different rocks as you can)
- sheet of cardboard
- magnet

Rock out with your magnet—while learning about the importance of iron in **magnetic attraction**!

WHAT'S THE SCIENCE?

Rocks are made up of many different types of minerals. Some rocks contain iron, which is magnetic. The iron in the rocks is what attracted them to your magnet.

Steps
1. Place the rocks on the cardboard. Spread them out.
2. Now place your magnet close to each of the rocks. What happens? Are some rocks more attracted to the magnet than others?

59 ★ BREAKFAST ROCKS

Do you have a favorite kind of cereal? Magnets do, too!

WHAT'S THE SCIENCE?

Objects containing iron are attracted to magnets. Most ready-to-eat cereals contain iron. Our bodies need iron to help carry **oxygen**, which helps fuel our bodies.

DID YOU KNOW?

Astronauts on Apollo 11 ate breakfast cereal that was mixed with fruit and pressed into cubes. Without **gravity**, it would be impossible to pour cereal (and milk) into a bowl!

Materials

- different cereal types
- cup
- plastic zip bags
- rolling pin
- magnet

Steps

1. Pour one cup of cereal into a plastic bag. Let out as much air as you can before sealing the bag. Repeat with other cereal types, each in its own bag.

2. Use the rolling pin to crush the cereal in each of the bags. Keep going until it is as close to powder as possible.

3. Hold a magnet near each bag. Does the cereal cling to the magnet?

60 SALTY PAINTING

Brush on the artwork—and then brush off the **salt**. Bravo! You've created a masterpiece!

WHAT'S THE SCIENCE?

Halite is most commonly known as rock salt. It is the mineral form of sodium chloride (or salt). One of the properties of salt is that it absorbs water. Found in lake beds and seas where the water has **evaporated** over time, halite has resulted in salt beds hundreds of meters thick!

Materials

- 1 cup of salt (you can also use Epsom salts)
- 1 cup of hot tap water
- pan
- 4 small bowls
- 3 different types of food coloring
- paintbrush
- large sheet of paper (you can use different colored sheets of construction paper if you like)

Steps

1. Place the salt and water in a pan and combine (get an adult to help you with this).

2. Divide the mixture into four small bowls. Use 4 drops of food coloring to color the paint, using one color per bowl. Leave one plain.

3. With the paint and brush, paint on the paper. When you finish, leave it to dry. The water dries, leaving the salt to make a crystal pattern on the paper.

---

61 LIFE'S A BEACH

Sedimentary rock can take years to form. Who has the time? Try this speedy alternative!

WHAT'S THE SCIENCE?

Sedimentary rock is made of layers that are packed together. When water that contains minerals comes into contact with the rock, it seeps between particles and then evaporates, leaving the minerals behind. These minerals cement the particles together, forming a larger rock.

Materials

- Epsom salts (Use 2 parts water to 1 part salt)
- water
- bowl
- sand
- paper cup
- magnifying glass

Steps

1. Mix the salts and water together in a bowl to form "cement."

2. Pour sand into the paper cup, filling it halfway. Pack the sand down using your hand.

3. Slowly pour in the "cement" to fill the cup.

4. Leave the cup somewhere warm while the sand dries. Depending on the weather or temperature, this can take one to three days.

5. Slowly and carefully, tear away the paper cup.

6. Use the magnifying glass to observe the sand.

SUPER SANDPAPER

Materials

- sheet of A4 paper
- glue
- sand
- strainer (optional)

Never underestimate the power of tiny grains of sand—they can do amazing things!

WHAT'S THE SCIENCE?

When sand is blown against Earth's surfaces, such as cliffs and mountains, it changes their shape. Blowing sand also breaks down rock on unprotected sand dunes—dislodging surface sand and sometimes even causing sandstorms.

Steps

1. Spread your piece of paper out flat.
2. Lightly cover the paper with glue.
3. While the glue is still wet, cover the paper with sand. (You could use a strainer to do this if you want to spread the sand evenly.)
4. Leave the glue to dry. When it is dry, test your sandpaper by sanding a piece of wood.

CRYSTAL CUTOUTS

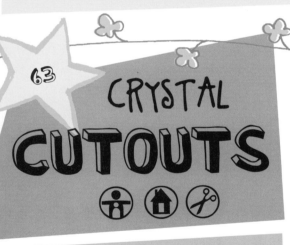

Materials

- photocopier
- scissors
- glitter
- glue
- cord or strong string for necklace

You already know that gemstones are beautiful—but do you know how they get their sparkle?

WHAT'S THE SCIENCE?

Most gemstones are formed beneath Earth's surface. Emeralds form when rainwater or water from cooling magma mixes with minerals. Magmatic gems, such as topazes and rubies, form when magma crystallizes.

Steps

1. Photocopy this page.
2. Cut out the shapes along the solid lines.
3. Fold the tabs inward and match them to their corresponding crystal faces.
4. Decorate the crystals with glue and glitter if you'd like.
5. String the gems onto the cord or string.

64 CRYSTAL CREATIONS

OK, so Mother Nature can do some cool stuff, like making crystals—but so can you!

WHAT'S THE SCIENCE?

Crystals are minerals; they form when the liquid rock inside Earth cools and hardens into a regular geological matrix, or pattern. Most of Earth's crystals were formed millions of years ago. Most mineral crystals take thousands of years to "grow." But not salt! Halite, or rock salt, will grow right before your eyes.

DID YOU KNOW?

Gems get their color from the minerals they form from. Out of all of the minerals in the world, there are only a few that produce the beautiful colors of gems.

Materials

- 2–3 cups of water
- saucepan
- stove
- 1 lb (500 g) of Epsom salts
- bowl
- two pieces of charcoal

Steps

1. Warm up the water in the saucepan (you may want to ask an adult for help).

2. Stir the Epsom salts into the water until no more will **dissolve**.

3. Tip the water into the bowl and add the charcoal.

4. Now leave your bowl in a safe place and check it over the next five days. Have crystals formed in your dish?

65 MOCK ROCKS

Sometimes things are even cooler on the inside than out!

Materials

- Epsom salts
- 2 cups warm water
- eggshell halves
- food coloring (different colors if possible)

Steps

1. Spoon Epsom salts into the cups of warm water until no more will dissolve.
2. Add food coloring to each cup of solution.
3. Pour the solution into the eggshell halves and leave the water to evaporate. (This may take a few days, so be patient.)
4. When the water has evaporated, you will have made your very own geodes!

WHAT'S THE SCIENCE?

Geodes are round stones with crystals in the middle. Sometimes the crystals inside can be different colors—this is because of the different minerals that are inside the rock.

---

66 SWEET TREATS

Crystals can be more than just beautiful—they can be delicious, too!

Materials

- dark colored plate
- 1 cup maple syrup
- saucepan
- stove

Steps

1. Chill the plate in the freezer for 30 minutes.
2. Ask an adult to help you heat the maple syrup in the saucepan over a medium heat.
3. Stir the syrup as it warms. Continue until it thickens and crystals begin forming on the bottom and sides of the saucepan.
4. Pour the syrup onto the cold plate and watch crystals form.

WHAT'S THE SCIENCE?

To make candy, sugar and water are combined at an extremely high temperature. Most of the water evaporates away, but most of the sugar remains in the liquid. What is left is a "supersaturated" solution. This means there is more sugar in the solution than what would be possible if it hadn't been heated. When the candy begins to cool, it begins to crystallize back into a solid. In nature, gemstones, stalagmites and stalactites are also formed by this crystallization process.

YOU GLOW, GIRL!

What's better than colorful crystals? Colorful crystals that glow in the dark, of course!

WHAT'S THE SCIENCE?

Geodes form when there is a hollow pocket in rock that allows crystals to form inside. These pockets can be left from air bubbles after a volcanic eruption.

She did it!

Kathleen Yardley Lonsdale
Ireland

Kathleen grew up in Ireland in the early 1900s. At the age of 16, Kathleen won a scholarship to go to college, where she studied **physics**. As soon as she left college, Kathleen began studying crystals. She proved that benzene (an important structure in **organic chemistry**) was a flat, regular hexagon! In 1949 she became Professor of Chemistry at London's University College. She was also the first woman ever to be President of the British Association for the Advancement of Science.

Materials

- egg
- glow-in-the-dark paint
- paintbrush
- 1 cup hot water
- small jug
- borax
- food coloring
- paper towel
- cup

Steps

1. Carefully tap the top of the egg against a counter top to crack it.
2. Discard the inside of the egg (or save it to cook and eat later).
3. Rinse the inside of the shell. If there is any interior membrane (the thin sac around the egg white) remaining, peel it off.
4. Let the shell air dry completely.
5. Paint the inside of the shell with glow-in-the-dark paint, then set it aside to dry.
6. Pour the hot water into the jug, then stir in borax. Stop when the borax no longer dissolves and begins to solidify in the bottom of the jug.
7. Add a drop or two of food coloring.
8. Crumple the paper towel inside the cup to make a "nest," then sit the shell inside it.
9. Pour the crystal solution into the shell. Fill it as high as possible.
10. Wait several hours for the crystals to grow.
11. Tip the shell to remove excess solution, allowing the geode to dry.
12. Turn out the light and enjoy your glow-in-the-dark geode!

SPARKLE STRINGS

🔥 🏠 ✂️

Materials

- 1½ cups of water
- saucepan
- stove
- ¼ cup of salt (you can also use alum or sugar)
- narrow glass
- 12 in (30 cm) piece of string

Have you ever grown your own crystal?

WHAT'S THE SCIENCE?

When a substance such as salt or sugar is mixed in warm water, it dissolves. When the water evaporates, the substance remains, leaving behind solid crystals.

Steps

1. Warm the water in the saucepan on low heat (you may want to ask an adult for help).
2. Add salt to the water until no more will dissolve.
3. Leave this to cool until crystals form.
4. Take out the largest crystal and replace it with more salt.
5. Heat the solution again until the salt dissolves.
6. Cool the solution and pour it into the glass.
7. Tie the string around the crystal and place it in the solution. Leave it for a few days. What happens?

VOLCAN-OH-NO!

🔥 🏠 ✂️

Materials

- metal funnel
- modeling clay (you will only need a small amount)
- frying pan
- stove
- water

Hey, hot stuff! Get ready for this explosive experiment!

WHAT'S THE SCIENCE?

When pressure builds in a **magma chamber** beneath a volcano, this can cause fractures in Earth's crust, allowing magma to rise to the surface. As the pressure builds, the molten rock expands and bursts out of the vent at the top, releasing hot ash and **lava**.

Steps

1. Take the metal funnel and cover the narrow end with a very thin strip of modeling clay.
2. Fill the frying pan a third full of water, and place it on the stove to heat. (Ask an adult for help if you need it.)
3. Place the wide end of the funnel in the water.
4. Turn up the heat and stand clear!

MAGICAL MÂCHÉ

This papier-mâché volcano takes time and patience—but the result is guaranteed magic!

WHAT'S THE SCIENCE?

Magma contains gases that escape as the magma flows to the surface. These gas bubbles can escape slowly or can erupt like an exploding fizzy drink. If the magma is runny, the lava flows outward and bubbles move slowly. If the magma is thicker, it cannot flow easily—and instead, the gases burst out in a violent eruption.

Materials

- plastic soda bottle
- tape
- empty cardboard box
- newspaper
- scissors
- papier-mâché solution (a mixture of water and glue)
- dark gray, black, and red paint
- paintbrush
- 2 tablespoons baking soda
- red food coloring
- drinking glass
- ¼ cup vinegar

DID YOU KNOW?

The word "volcano" comes from the name of the Roman god of fire—Vulcan!

Steps

1. Remove the lid from the bottle. Keeping the bottle open side up, tape the base of the bottle to the bottom of the upside-down box.

2. Loosely crumple several sheets of newspaper into balls.

3. Tape the balls to the sides of the bottle and around the base, making a mountain.

4. Cut strips of newspaper and dip each strip into the papier-mâché solution.

5. Slide your finger down each strip to remove any excess solution. Now stick the strips to your "volcano," covering it completely, but keeping the opening at the top clear.

6. Allow the volcano to dry overnight.

7. When the volcano is completely dry, paint it. Use the red paint to make lava, the gray paint for the body of the volcano and the black for the ash.

8. Once the paint is dry, your volcano is ready to erupt! Pour the baking soda into the bottle, filling it about a quarter of the way.

9. Drop some food coloring into the glass, then add the vinegar. Now pour this mixture into the volcano—and stand back!

71 ICE, ICE BABY

Turn frosting into lava— and watch it flow!

Materials

- 1 lb (500 g) of frosting/icing
- 2 bowls
- fridge
- 2 plates

Steps

1. Divide the frosting/icing evenly between the two bowls.
2. Put one of the bowls in the fridge until the frosting has cooled but can still be poured.
3. Now pour the warm mixture onto one of the plates, and the cool mixture onto the other. What do you notice about how the frosting pours?

WHAT'S THE SCIENCE?

The pressure, heat, and flow of magma determine what type of igneous rock is formed. Igneous rock formed from slow-flowing lava at the Earth's surface will have a different structure to, for example, lava that erupted under the sea in cold water. **Pumice** is an igneous rock that forms from extremely hot and pressurized "frothy" lava, making holes in the rock. **Obsidian** or "black glass" is formed when the cooling lava does not flow quickly and instantly hardens.

72 GROOVY GRAVY

Time to make dinner? Make your specialty—volcanic mud!

Materials

- gravy mix
- water
- saucepan
- stove

WHAT'S THE SCIENCE?

Mud volcanoes are small cones of mud shaped like volcanoes. When gas rises through the ground, it dissolves rock—and makes mud. With a mud volcano, hot mud does not simply boil; it flows much like lava. Sometimes it even explodes in the air! Eruptions are caused when the pressure from underground gases builds up and bursts out of the mud.

Steps

1. Mix your gravy mix with some water in a saucepan. (Check the recipe on the packet for quantities.)
2. Place the saucepan on the stove and turn on the heat (ask an adult for help if you need it).
3. What happens? Can you see bubbles rising to the surface?

73 SUPER SINKERS

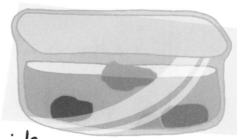

All rocks sink, right? Right ... ?

WHAT'S THE SCIENCE?

Rocks can float or sink depending on their **density** and **porosity**. Density is the amount of matter something has, and porosity describes how much space there is between the matter. More porous rocks, with less dense material between the spaces, are more likely to float.

Materials

- pen and paper
- clear plastic container filled with water
- pumice stone
- small piece each of sandstone and granite
- small brick or piece of cement

Steps

1. First, predict which rocks you think will float and which rocks will sink. Write your predictions down.
2. Drop all of your rocks into the water.
3. Check how many you got right.

74 THIRSTY ROCKS!

Do rocks really get thirsty?

WHAT'S THE SCIENCE?

Igneous rocks are formed when lava or magma cools. Often air bubbles are trapped inside the lava or magma during the cooling process. The more porous rocks with lots of air bubbles absorb the most water because there's more space to fill. Pumice is a good example of a rock that is filled with air.

Materials

- 4 large, clear plastic containers
- measuring jug
- water
- pen and paper
- one piece each of granite, sandstone, pumice, and limestone

Steps

1. Measure and pour an equal amount of water into each container. Note the amount.
2. Put one rock into the middle of each container. Make sure the water covers the rocks completely. Leave the rocks in the water for at least 30 minutes. Do the water levels change?
3. Carefully remove the rocks, allowing the excess water to drain back into each container. Make a note of which rock was in each container.
4. Now calculate how much water each rock soaked up. Pour the remaining water back into the measuring container and subtract that amount from the original amount poured.

ROCK-A-BYE!

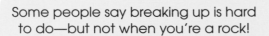

Some people say breaking up is hard to do—but not when you're a rock!

WHAT'S THE SCIENCE?

When water inside rock freezes, it expands, causing the rock to crack. After several cycles of freezing and thawing, the rock will begin to break up.

DID YOU KNOW?

Freeze-thaw is the process in which water inside rocks freezes and expands. As the water expands the rock will crack. This cycle will repeat several times until a break occurs.

Materials

- variety of found rocks, including cement or paving stone
- pen and paper
- plastic bottle
- water
- freezer

Steps

1. Study the rocks you have collected. Write down which one you think will break down the most when you freeze it.

2. Put the rocks in the plastic bottle. Fill the bottle with water and freeze it.

3. When the water has frozen, take the bottle out and let the water thaw.

4. Once the ice has melted completely, put the bottle back into the freezer. Repeat this cycle five times.

5. After the fifth time, remove the rocks from the bottle. Which have changed the most? Which have lost small particles?

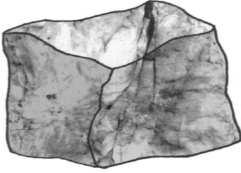

CHALK IT UP!

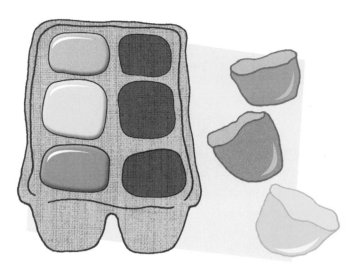

Can't find the right color chalk? Make your own!

WHAT'S THE SCIENCE?

Chalk is actually a very soft kind of rock. It is made of a material called calcium carbonate—the same material that limestone is made of. Chalk is soft and usually white or yellow.

DID YOU KNOW?

Chalk can form anything from a small deposit to a giant cliff, such as the White Cliffs of Dover in the United Kingdom.

Materials

- plastic gloves and dust mask
- stick for mixing (one you can throw away when you are finished with it)
- 2 cups plaster of Paris
- 1 cup water
- large mixing bowl (preferably disposable)
- 4 tablespoons tempera paint (one color is fine; more for more colorful chalk)
- egg carton

Steps

1. Put on the gloves and mask.
2. Use the stick to mix the plaster of Paris and water in the bowl. Mix until it is stiff and creamy.
3. Add the tempera paint to the plaster. If you want your chalk to have a solid color, stir it well. If you would prefer your chalk to have a marbled appearance, stir briefly instead. For a very marbled appearance, use two or more colors of paint.
4. Pour the plaster into the egg carton wells and leave to harden.
5. Once the plaster has hardened (approximately half an hour), remove the chalk from the wells.
6. It will take up to a day for the chalk to dry completely—but you can use it as soon as it has been removed from the carton!

ANCIENT ART

Mix up some paint, grab a rock, and make some ancient art!

WHAT'S THE SCIENCE?

Most paints we use these days are made from chemicals, but paints can also be made using natural materials, such as animal fat, dirt, rocks, and minerals. Ancient rock paintings can still be seen because they were made in sheltered areas such as caves, so were not exposed to weathering.

Materials

← CHALK IS A SEDIMENTARY ROCK!

- stick of chalk
- 2 resealable plastic freezer bags
- hammer
- clean glass jar
- popsicle/icy pole stick
- water
- yolk of 1 egg
- bowl
- rock
- paintbrush

Steps

1. Put the chalk inside one of the plastic bags. Seal it, then put it inside the second plastic bag and seal that bag, too. Make sure you remove as much air from the bags as you can before sealing.
2. Hammer the chalk until it becomes a fine powder.
3. Pour the powder into the jar.
4. Using the popsicle/icy pole stick, stir in a teaspoon of water until you have a smooth paste.
5. Add the egg yolk (it will act as a binder) and stir.
6. Mix in some water, a bit at a time, until your paste has a paint-like consistency to it. Now grab your rock and paintbrush and create your own rock painting!

78 ROCK WRITING

Writing on paper is so last year—try writing on clay!

WHAT'S THE SCIENCE?

Clay is a combination of different minerals that are rich in **alumina**, **silica**, and water. When clay is wet, it is described as "plastic", meaning its shape is easy to alter. When clay is fired at high temperatures, it loses its water and becomes as hard as stone.

Materials

- 1 cup flour (plus a little extra for sifting)
- 1 cup salt
- ½ cup hot water
- bowl
- spoon
- cutting board
- food coloring
- rolling pin
- rock

SCIENCE ROCKS

Steps

1. Mix the flour, salt, and hot water in the bowl.
2. Sprinkle flour over the cutting board.
3. Knead the dough on the board for at least five minutes. Mix in food coloring.
4. Roll the dough into a flat tablet.
5. Use the rock to write a message on your tablet, then allow it to dry (it will take between one and five days, depending on its size).

79 ROCK THE GARDEN

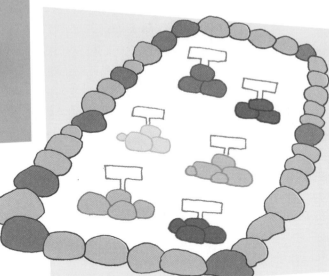

Who said gardens are only for things that grow? Think outside the box with this rad rock garden!

WHAT'S THE SCIENCE?

Geologists study the chemistry and physics of Earth's crust. They learn about all different kinds of rocks, and use them to understand more about Earth's history.

Materials

- rock reference materials
- a container or strong bag
- strong paper and pen
- popsicle/icy pole sticks
- glue

DID YOU KNOW?

Japanese rock gardens are often called "Zen gardens." They can often be found at Zen temples designed for meditation.

Steps

1. Gather some references about different kinds of rocks—try a book store, a library, or the Internet.
2. Using a container or strong bag, begin collecting the different rocks you see.
3. Wash or dust off the rocks so you can see them more clearly.
4. Using your reference materials, see how many you can identify.
5. Use the rocks you cannot identify to create a border for your rock garden.
6. "Plant" the rocks you have identified by arranging them in rows, circles, or any shape you'd like. Be sure that the same kinds of rocks are grouped together.
7. Use the paper, pen, popsicle/icy pole sticks, and glue to create name signs for each rock group.
8. Plant the signs in your garden to tell your visitors which rocks are on display.

80 SHINE A LIGHT

Gemstones are destined to light up any room!
But how do they respond to light?

WHAT'S THE SCIENCE?

Some rocks and minerals are transparent, meaning light passes through them. Transparent objects are referred to as "diaphanous." Other minerals are opaque, which means light cannot pass through the surface. Translucent materials are in between opaque and transparent ones. They are slightly denser than transparent objects, but not as dense as opaque ones. They only allow for some light rays to pass through. Diaphaneity and color are good indicators of a mineral's type.

Materials

- gemstone reference materials
- collected gemstones (such as quartz and emerald)
- bright light

Steps

1. Find out what gemstones are common to your area. Quartz is easy to come by: look out for a 6-sided crystal, which is common quartz (or silicon dioxide). Emeralds are common gemstones in jewelry.

2. Collect as many gemstones as you can. Look outside on the ground and indoors for objects made of rock. Consult the Internet or a book about gems to see if any of the rocks you found are indeed gemstones.

3. Shine a bright light at each gemstone, one at a time. If the light enters and exits, the gemstone is translucent or transparent. If the light is unable to penetrate the gemstone's surface, it is opaque.

81 GLOWING GEMS

Gemstones are a hot item at any great party. Find some to brighten up your outfit—and then rock out all night!

WHAT'S THE SCIENCE?

Some gemstones glow under **ultraviolet light** (or UV light). When you shine a black light on them, they can display beautiful and spooky colors. Calcite, a gemstone, **fluoresces** in four different colors—red, pink, yellow, and blue.

Materials

- collected gemstones
- gemstone reference materials
- paper
- pen
- black light (globes available at specialty lighting and hardware stores)

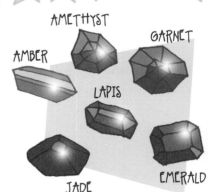

AMETHYST
GARNET
AMBER
LAPIS
JADE
EMERALD

Steps

1. Use the gemstones you collected for the previous experiment (experiment 80.)

2. Arrange the gemstones in a row. Using the reference materials, mark down the order you've arranged them on a piece of paper.

3. Turn off the lights and shine the black light on the gemstones, one at a time. Which ones glow? Write down the results.

MUD BUD

This experiment will change your mind about playing in mud!

WHAT'S THE SCIENCE?

Geologists study rocks and Earth. They search for fossils, which are animals and plants that lived thousands of years ago, and that have been preserved in rocks. The condition of the fossils and their impressions give us clues about what Earth used to be like.

Materials

- soil
- water
- seashell
- wax paper
- cookie sheet/baking tray

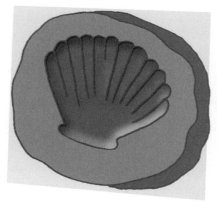

Steps

1. Mix together soil and water until you have thick mud.
2. Stir in the shell.
3. Spread out the wax paper on top of the cookie sheet/baking tray. Pour the mud over it.
4. Shape the mud into a "mud pie." Make sure the shell is completely hidden.
5. Leave the cookie sheet in the sun for 1–2 days, until the mud dries.
6. Gently break the piece of mud to find your fossil. Observe the imprint it left behind.

SHAKE IT UP!

Make a rock tumbler—and then shake it up, like the rock star you are!

WHAT'S THE SCIENCE?

Eroding the surface of a rock makes it smooth and shiny. Ever heard the expression "diamond in the rough?" Even the most precious minerals have to have their surfaces eroded and smoothed in order make attractive jewelry.

Materials

- a very soft rock (one with a rating of 5–7 on **Mohs scale of hardness**, such as apatite, orthoclase, and quartz)
- plastic cylindrical container with a lid
- sand
- water

Steps

1. Put the rock into the container. Add sand and water, filling it three-quarters of the way. Secure the lid on the container.
2. Shake the container as often as possible, for a week or more, keeping it closed.
3. Open the container and remove the rock. Is it different?
4. Reseal the container and continue shaking and checking on the rock over time. How does it continue to change?

84 THE ACID TEST

Try this experiment—and become the ultimate fizz whiz!

Materials

- bowl
- vinegar
- one piece each of granite, sandstone, and limestone
- tongs

Steps

1. Fill the bowl with vinegar.
2. Place the granite in the vinegar. What happens? Remove the granite with the tongs.
3. Next, place the sandstone in the vinegar. What happens? Remove the sandstone.
4. Finally, place the limestone in the vinegar. What happens? Does it fizz?

WHAT'S THE SCIENCE?

Some minerals react to acids; others don't react at all. Limestone gives off a gas when it comes in contact with vinegar. Limestone can be made from fused shells, coral, and bones of marine life. These are made of calcium carbonate—a substance that forms from the mineral calcite. When exposed to a weak acid, like vinegar, it produces **carbon dioxide**.

85 ROCK AROUND THE CLOCK

One rock is definitely cool. A group of rocks, however—well it rocks!

Materials

- rock collection
- pen
- paper

Steps

1. Go outside or to a nearby park or beach.
2. Collect six rocks, making sure they are all collected from different areas (a garden bed, next to a lake, or from the school oval, for example).
3. Write down all the differences that you can spot between the rocks.
4. Do you think that the different locations where the rocks were found could account for any of the differences identified?

WHAT'S THE SCIENCE?

Geologists know that rocks found in specific places can have unique qualities. For example, willemite from New Jersey's Franklin Caves contains **manganese**—a special **element**. These rocks always glow under UV light. Rocks can help tell the story of the place where they were found.

ROCK MY WORLD

86

How many things in your world ROCK?

WHAT'S THE SCIENCE?

Rocks, metals, and minerals are some of our most important **natural resources**. You can find gold in computers, aluminum in cans, marble counter tops, slate tables, pumice stones for feet, talcum powder ... you name it!

Materials

- paper
- pen

Steps

1. Think about how many items in your home might be made of rock or metal. Take a guess.
2. Now walk slowly through each room, examining and touching every object you can.
3. How many objects did you find that were made from rock? How many were made from metal? Are there more than you had guessed? Do any of your findings surprise you?

87

GOING FOR THE GOLD

Ready to strike it lucky? Go for gold!

WHAT'S THE SCIENCE?

Gold is a precious metal that can be found in riverbeds. Gold is heavier than rock or sand, so it sinks to the bottom. Panning for gold involves scooping up dirt from the riverbed and swishing away the rock and sand with water to reveal any gold.

Materials

- flat tray
- water
- birdseed
- colander or sieve
- gold paint

Steps

1. Fill the tray with water to a shallow level.
2. Pour the birdseed into the water.
3. Use your colander to scoop some of the birdseed out of the water.
4. Shake your colander so that the small particles fall through the holes while the larger ones remain. Pick out a particular type of seed. This is your pretend gold.
5. Repeat the process until you have a pile of seeds.
6. When you have finished, take the pile of seeds and paint them gold. The wet paint will bind them together in small clusters. For larger nuggets, glue the seeds together. When the paint has dried, pan for your "real" gold.

EXTRA! EXTRA!

Some rocks are truly out of this world!

Materials

- large piece of white paper
- magnet
- magnifying glass

WHAT'S THE SCIENCE?

Extraterrestrial rocks are usually dark, round particles, often with pitted surfaces. Each day, tons of these particles break off from larger **meteorites** and fall to Earth. They are extremely common in space and are easier to find in the polar regions, where they don't combine with other sediments. You won't feel them or see them unless you look very carefully—they are miniscule, which is why they are called "micrometeorites."

Steps

1. Go outside on a sunny day (the experiment won't work if it rains) and secure your piece of paper to an area that is out in the open.
2. Leave the paper there for 4–6 hours.
3. Collect the paper carefully. Make sure that anything you have collected rolls into the middle of the paper.
4. Hold your magnet under the paper and lightly shake off the material gathered. The material not attracted to your magnet will just fall off.
5. Collect the material that did not fall off and look at it through a magnifying glass.

She did it!

Florence Bascom
United States of America

Having been interested in the subject since she was a young girl, Florence studied geology at college. She then went on to take graduate school classes in science. She was required to sit behind a screen to ensure she didn't disrupt the males in the room! Florence also became a college professor, and was the first woman ever hired by the US Geological Survey. She also trained many women who would go on to revolutionize the role of women in science.

89 BRICK TRICKS

Make it—and then break it!

WHAT'S THE SCIENCE?

Bricks are one of the strongest building materials used by humans. They can be made from clay, concrete, shale, or slate. But true bricks are made through a process of heating and then cooling raw clay. Adding materials such as grass or straw helps bind the brick together and lets it dry more evenly.

Materials

- soil
- water
- sand
- dried leaves or grass
- small twigs
- dirt
- straw
- ice cube tray
- pen, paper, and tape
- hammer

Steps

1. Mix the soil and water together in several different batches to make different types of mud. Add different "ingredients" to each batch—make one with the sand, one with the dried leaves, one with the straw and so on. There should be a variety of consistencies.

2. Pour a sample from each batch of mud into the ice cube tray. Label each of your "bricks" with what it was mixed with.

3. Leave the tray in the sun for 2–3 days.

4. Predict which brick you think will be the strongest. Remove the bricks from the trays and test each with a hammer.

90 LIFE'S A BEACH

Life's a beach—and guess what? So is this experiment!

Materials

- hammer
- small rocks and shells
- plastic container
- aquarium gravel
- blue food coloring
- jug of water

WHAT'S THE SCIENCE?

Sand and rocks are moved by waves. When waves crash, they bang rocks together, wearing them down. This type of water erosion produces sand. Water and wind also displace sand, forming beaches and dunes.

Steps

1. Using your hammer, tap on the rocks and shells to make them into a fine "sand."

2. Pour your sand into a plastic container. Add an equal amount of aquarium gravel.

3. Add a few drops of blue food coloring to the jug of water. Pour some into the container—there should be about the same amount of water as there is sand.

4. Rock the container back and forth to demonstrate how waves form and wash over sand. How does the sand change as you tilt the container from side to side?

91 SOIL SUPPER

Are you ready to get all the dirt on soil layers?

Materials

- two different colored cakes
- crumbled chocolate cookies (such as Oreos)
- green candies or sprinkles
- chocolate-covered pretzel sticks

Steps

1. Lay one cake on top of the other. The bottom layer represents the rock base that lies below the soil, called bedrock. The second layer represents subsoil, which is full of clay and mineral deposits from layers above.

2. Layer the crumbled cookies on the cake. This represents topsoil, which is the layer with the most living materials, such as bacteria and worms. This is where seeds germinate and plant roots grow.

3. Sprinkle the green candies and pretzel sticks on top. These represent humus and leaf litter, which consists of broken plants, leaves, twigs, and other material.

WHAT'S THE SCIENCE?

Soil can take up to 1000 years to form from decomposing material and weathered rock. Scientists recognize many soil types by analyzing their layers. The top layers of soil are made up of material before they have decomposed, as well as humus (the rich soil formed when decomposed matter combines with sediments). Below this are several more layers sitting on top of bedrock: the solid rock at the bottom of the soil layer.

92 QUICK STICK

This experiment is quick to make—but not a trap!

Materials

- 1 cup corn flour (corn starch)
- ½ cup water
- plastic container
- spoon

Steps

1. Mix the corn flour (corn starch) and water in your container.

2. Stir it slowly and gently, then turn your container upside down and allow the solution to drip, which shows that it is a liquid.

3. Now stir the solution quickly. Poke it with the end of your spoon. Is the solution still liquid—or has it become solid?

WHAT'S THE SCIENCE?

Quicksand, a thick mixture of sand and water, is a natural phenomenon. It occurs when water **agitates** loose sand and becomes trapped inside of it. The resulting **liquefied** soil is unable to support any weight. Quicksand is not a liquid—but it behaves like one by flowing and losing its rigid shape.

DID YOU KNOW?

Quicksand is rarely deeper than a few feet.

93 PRESS TO IMPRESS

Make your own fossils—and impress your friends!

Materials

- 1 cup of coffee grounds
- ½ cup of cold coffee
- 1 cup of flour
- ½ cup of salt
- bowl
- wax paper
- small objects (fossils) such as shells, rocks, sticks, and coins

Steps

1. Mix together the coffee grounds, cold coffee, flour, and salt in a bowl.
2. Turn your "dough" out onto a sheet of wax paper, and knead it until it softens.
3. Press your "fossils" into the dough to create impressions, then remove your fossils and leave the dough to dry overnight.

WHAT'S THE SCIENCE?

Paleontologists study impressions made by dinosaurs and ancient organisms to better understand when, how, and where they lived. The impressions are found in blocks of mud that hardened and turned to stone. The clearest impressions are found in areas that suffered the least weathering over the past 65 million years!

94 PERFECT PRINTS

Make a fabulous footprint by following these simple steps!

WHAT'S THE SCIENCE?

Fossils are frequently found in sedimentary rock. Many were created by animals and plants that were buried or trapped in sediment. As the sediment hardens, it turns into rock—and the animals and plants become fossils.

Materials

- empty two-liter milk or juice carton
- scissors
- bucket of sand
- small cup
- large cup
- plaster
- water

Steps

1. Carefully cut a milk carton lengthwise.
2. Fill the milk carton with a layer of sand about 2 1/2 in (6 cm) deep.
3. Place one foot on top of the sand, and carefully press down so that your footprint remains on the sand.
4. Pour 1 cup of plaster into the larger cup. Add ½ cup of water and let the mixture sit until all of the water has been absorbed. The plaster will be your pretend mud that is needed in the fossilization process.
5. After the plaster has been mixed, carefully pour it into the milk carton. Make sure to completely cover the footprint with plaster.
6. After the plaster has set, carefully lift your fossilized footprint out of the sand and give it a quick clean. Now you can compare your plaster fossil to the original footprint.

FOOTPRINT FINDER

Follow the footprints to find out who—or what!—was lurking nearby!

WHAT'S THE SCIENCE?

Footprints are impressions left by animals or people. Footprints can be found in rocks, dirt, mud, and snow. Scientists consider the size of a human footprint represents approximately 15% of a person's height. Many animal prints are nearly identical, making it a challenge to distinguish between them!

Steps

1. Go outside to your garden bed or to a nearby park or the beach, and look for footprints in the soil or sand.

2. Pour 1 cup of plaster into the larger cup. Add ½ cup of water and let the mixture sit until all of the water has been absorbed.

3. Carefully pour the plaster into your footprint. Make sure you completely cover the footprint.

4. After the plaster has set, carefully lift up your fossilized footprint. Now you have a record of the original footprint you found.

Materials

- small cup
- large cup
- plaster
- water

DID YOU KNOW?

To study footprints, scientists make castings by pouring liquid into a mold and allowing the liquid to solidify. Then they eject the cast from the mold so they can study it.

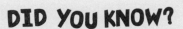

WONDER WORDS

agitates—Causes to move with an irregular or violent force.

alumina—Alumina, or aluminum oxide, is a common substance found in nature and in manufacturing. Rubies, for example, are made of alumina and other impurities such as chromium.

carbon dioxide—A colorless gas, containing one carbon atom and two oxygen atoms. It plays an important role in many chemical reactions, such as photosynthesis and cellular respiration. It also makes up a small part of Earth's atmosphere.

core—The center of Earth. Earth's core is made up of two layers, the inner and outer cores. Both the inner and outer core are full of iron and nickel, but the outer core is liquid, while the inner is solid, and about the size of the moon. Both reach extremely hot temperatures and cause Earth to have a magnetic field.

crust—The outermost layer of Earth, also known as the lithosphere. Earth's crust is made up of solid rock and soil, and topped with a vast ocean. It is thin under the sea (about 3–6 mi, or 5–10 km) and thicker under where continents lie (about 20–30 mi, or 30–50 km).

density—The measure of mass per unit of volume.

dissolve—The process by which a solid, liquid, or gas become incorporated into a liquid to form a solution.

element—A type of atom, such as oxygen, gold, neon, or carbon. There are 118 known varieties.

erosion—The process by which something is worn or ground down. Erosion of Earth's surface, such as landforms, mountains, and river beds, can be caused by gravity, ice, water, and wind.

evaporate—Change from a liquid into a gas.

extraterrestrial—Originating or existing beyond Earth or its atmosphere.

fluoresces—Emits light when exposed to radiation from another source.

geodes—Hollow rocks with cavities that are lined with crystals or other mineral matter.

geologists—Scientists who study the history of Earth, particularly through rocks. Geologists study Earth's formation, its composition, and its processes.

glacier—A large and slowly-moving mass of ice.

global warming—An increase in Earth's average temperature, caused by a build-up of greenhouse gases, which trap heat in Earth's atmosphere, causing changes to the climate.

gravity—A force of attraction between atoms. The greater an object's mass, the stronger its gravitational pull.

igneous rock—Rock formed when volcanic lava cools, such as obsidian.

iron—A heavy, magnetic metallic element that is silver-white in its pure state but that rusts easily in moist air. Iron can be found in meteorites and most igneous rocks. It is the most commonly used of all metals.

lava—Molten rock that is expelled from a volcano during eruption and then forms igneous rock as it hardens.

liquefied—Changed into a liquid state.

magma—Molten rock that lies beneath Earth's crust and that is under high pressure. Magma sometimes becomes lava when it emerges through volcanoes or hydrothermal vents.

magma chamber—A cavity or "pool" of molten rock that lies below Earth's surface and is linked to the surface by vents, which lead to volcanoes.

magnetic—A property of matter that causes the electrons in a material to line up with other magnets, such as when the electrons in iron line up with the magnetic orientation of Earth, and cause opposite poles to attract one another.

magnetic attraction—The attraction of opposite magnetic poles, north to south.

manganese—A brittle metallic element that can be found worldwide, but is most common on the ocean floor.

mantle—The middle layer of Earth. Almost 1865 mi (3000 km) thick, the mantle is made up of both semi-solid and molten rock.

metamorphic rock—Rock formed by the heat and pressure put on other types of rock. Slate and marble are examples of metamorphic rock.

meteorites—Meteors that come into contact with Earth's surface.

minerals—Minerals are substances formed in Earth's crust that have a regular chemical composition and recognizable physical properties. Some minerals are made up of one element, others of many molecules.

Mohs scale of hardness—Used to measure how hard a mineral is compared to other minerals or hard substances. It is used to help identify rocks.

natural resources—Parts of our natural system, such as water, forests, minerals, or soil, that we use.

nickel—A hard, silver-white metallic element that is resistant to corrosion and weakly magnetic.

north pole—The point where Earth's axis rotates. It is at 90 degrees north, or a perfect right angle, from the equator.

obsidian—"Black glass" that is formed when the cooling lava does not flow quickly, and instantly hardens.

organic chemistry—The science of organic compounds, which are solid, liquid, or gas compounds whose their molecules contain carbon.

oxygen—A colorless, odorless, tasteless gas that makes up about one-fifth of Earth's atmosphere and can be found in water and most rocks and minerals.

physics—The study of matter and its interaction with forces.

polar ice caps—Massive, dome-shaped sheets of ice that cover large areas (often land).

porosity—The degree to which an object is capable of absorbing liquids.

pumice—An igneous rock that forms from extremely hot and pressurized "frothy" lava. The bubbles in the lava make holes in the rock.

react—To transform a one set of chemical agents into another, caused by the electrons in the agents forming and breaking chemical bonds (the attraction between atoms).

rock cycle—The "life cycle" of a rock. It describes how rocks can change from one type to another, and how rock in Earth's crust is constantly changing and recycling.

salt—A substance that is the result of the neutralizing reaction of an acid and a base.

sedimentary rock—Rock formed when sediments accumulate and bond together, such as sandstone.

sediments—Materials that have been broken down by weathering and erosion.

silica—Commonly known as glass, this is the most common mineral on Earth. It also makes up sand, and the mineral quartz.

South pole—The point where Earth's axis rotates. It is at 90 degrees south, or a perfect right angle, from the equator.

tectonic plates—Big segments of Earth's crust that move and create mountains, oceanic trenches, and landforms on Earth. There are seven main tectonic plates.

ultraviolet light—Radiation that has wavelengths shorter than visible light. Some insects can see ultraviolet light and it can be seen indirectly, as it makes white objects fluoresce.

GO GREEN
ENVIRONMENTAL SCIENCES

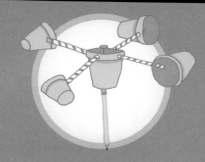

96 BUBBLE BREATH

Get down and dirty and find out if soil breathes!

Materials
- dry topsoil
- large bowl
- water that has been boiled and cooled (ask an adult to help)

Steps
1. Put the soil into the bowl.
2. Cover the soil with the water.
3. What happens? Do you notice bubbles in the water?

DID YOU KNOW?
There is air in soil—but not enough for you to be able to breathe under there!

WHAT'S THE SCIENCE?
Healthy soil needs to contain air so **organisms** in soil can survive. The organisms break down plants and **decompose** dead materials, keeping the soil healthy. Worms create holes in the soil, helping to **aerate** it.

97 WATER WASTE

Learning about erosion is definitely NOT a waste of time!

Materials
- drinking glass
- water
- two clear flat patches of loose soil

DID YOU KNOW?
America's Grand Canyon is a perfect example of a hole that was created by erosion over a long period of time. It is 6000 ft (1800 m) deep at its deepest point!

Steps
1. Fill your glass with water. Hold it about 6 in (15 cm) above the ground and pour the water onto the first patch of soil. Note what happens.
2. Now fill your glass again. Pour the water onto the second patch of soil, this time from a height of about 12 in (30 cm). Did the water affect the soil differently?

WHAT'S THE SCIENCE?
When water flows over land it **erodes** it. The roots of trees and bushes help hold soil together, so when land is cleared, the soil erodes much more quickly. Soil erosion is a big environmental problem.

DUNE
TRICKS

Could water have the power to bring down a whole mountain?

WHAT'S THE SCIENCE?

When there are green spaces in the city or a densely forested area in the country, rain is absorbed by the soil and used by plants. Without the plants, the rain is more likely to run off the surface of the soil, and erode the land as a result.

DID YOU KNOW?

*Soil erosion is a worldwide environmental problem with up to 80 percent of the world's agricultural soils affected. Erosion causes **sediments** to build up in waterways, as well as causing **habitats** to be lost in **wetland** areas.*

Materials

- 3 cups of sand
- 3 pans or plastic containers
- styrofoam cup
- pencil
- jug of water
- tissue

Steps

1. Tip one cup of sand into the middle of each pan.
2. Shape two of the piles of sand into small mountains. Smooth the third pile so that it covers the whole pan.
3. Predict what would happen to the sand in each pan if rain fell on it.
4. Make a small hole in the bottom of the styrofoam cup with a pencil. Place your finger over the hole, then half-fill the cup with water.
5. Hold the cup approximately 12 in (30 cm) above the center of your smooth pan. Move your finger so that the water trickles out. Observe what happens.
6. Repeat the same procedure on one of the mountains of sand. Observe the results.
7. Cover your third mountain with the tissue—this represents plants growing on the mountain. Pour half the cup of water over the tissue-covered mountain, letting some water trickle out.
8. How does the shape of the land affect the amount of erosion? Does the tissue covering the mountain make a difference?

99 LISTEN **UP!**

Sure, music is fun to listen to—but did you know that plants like it, too?

WHAT'S THE SCIENCE?

Some people believe that certain kinds of music can help plants grow. Scientists can test theories such as this by collecting and recording information and analyzing the results.

Materials

- three identical plants, of the same type and size
- two music players, such as a radio, computer, or CD player

Steps

1. Place one plant next to a music player that is playing classical music. Place one next to a music player that is playing rock music. Put the last plant in a quiet place.

2. Take care of the plants, making sure they get the same amount of water and sunlight, for two weeks. Be sure that the plants near the music have music playing beside them for the same amount of time each day.

3. After two weeks, compare the three plants. Did the plants with music grow better? Did the kind of music make any difference?

100 SNIP **TIPS**

Don't like the color of your flower? Easy—change it!

WHAT'S THE SCIENCE?

When you water a plant, the water goes into the soil. The plant's roots draw the water out of the soil and carry it up the stem of the plant. Special tubes in the stem take the water to the leaves and new shoots.

Materials

- water
- cup
- food coloring (blue or red)
- carnation
- scissors

Steps

1. Pour water into the cup until it is three-quarters full.

2. Add 3–5 drops of food coloring.

3. Trim the end of the carnation's stem, then place it in the water.

4. Leave the flower in the water for five days. Watch how its petals change.

5. Remove the flower from the cup. Turn it upside down and examine the stem. What do you notice about its **pores**?

101 SIMPLY SCENTSATIONAL

Learning how to **extract** oils from flowers is sweet science at its best!

WHAT'S THE SCIENCE?

Some flowers have great smelling oils that can be collected by steaming and **distilling** the oil from the petals, such as rose and lavender. Some plants, however, do not have oils that can be extracted easily, or don't smell as nice once they are separated from the plant! Your nose knows!

Materials

- 4 cups of water
- saucepan with a lid
- two cups of flower petals (roses are best)
- spoon
- strainer
- two bowls
- big spoon
- red food coloring
- storage container, such as a small glass bottle

Steps

1. Pour the water into the saucepan. Cover it with a lid. Bring the water to a low boil.

2. Leave the saucepan on the stove, but turn off the heat. Remove the lid and pour the petals into the water. Stir with a spoon.

3. Return the lid to the saucepan. Leave for a few hours.

4. Remove the lid and strain the saucepan over a bowl. Press on the petals with the back of a big spoon, squeezing out as much liquid as you can.

5. Add a drop of red food coloring, so the perfume takes on a pink hue, and pour the perfume into the bottle.

102 PRETTY PRESSINGS

Flowers don't have to fade away—turn them into art and keep them forever!

WHAT'S THE SCIENCE?

Flowers get their color from **pigments** in the petals. Carotenoids (ke-rot-enn-oyds) and anthocyanins (an-thuh-sy-uh-nens) are different kinds of pigments that can create all the colors of the rainbow. Once the flower has been dried, water cannot cause it to decompose, so it keeps its color.

Materials

- fresh, brightly colored flowers
- paper
- heavy books

Steps

1. Make sure the flowers are not wet.

2. Place a sheet of paper on a book, then put some flowers on the paper. Make sure they're not touching each other or they won't dry properly.

3. Place another sheet of paper on top of the flowers, then place another book on top. Repeat with more layers of paper, flowers, paper, and books, until you have run out of flowers.

4. Put the "flower press" somewhere it won't be knocked over, and leave for at least four weeks.

103 GARDEN GAUGE

Rainy days don't have to give you the blues!

WHAT'S THE SCIENCE?

A rain gauge can help a scientist determine rainfall patterns. Because water is so important to all living things, the amount an area receives helps determine what kind of **ecosystem** it is. Rainforests receive up to 5.6 ft (1.7 m) of rain a year, but **polar** regions receive almost no rain, due to the cold temperatures where liquid water doesn't form. What is typical in your ecosystem?
Find out if your gauge agrees by keeping a record of your rainfall patterns.

Materials

- empty plastic 4-pt (2-l) bottle
- scissors
- sand
- water
- ruler
- tape

Steps

1. Cut the spout off the bottle (ask an adult for help) and set it aside.
2. Pour enough sand into the bottle so that it fills up the bumps at the bottom, resulting in a level surface to measure from. Add water until you can just see the water level above the sand.
3. Attach the ruler to the bottle. Make sure the "0" lines up with the water level.
4. Put the spout upside-down in the opening and tape it in place.
5. Set up your new rain gauge outside in an open area so it can catch the rain.
6. Record rainfall over time, emptying your gauge in between rainfalls.

DID YOU KNOW?

The record for the most rainfall in one year is held by Cherrapunji, India, where 85 ft (26 m) fell in 1860.

104 AIR CARE

Treat your plants with care—so we can have fresh air!

WHAT'S THE SCIENCE?

Plants need air to survive. Plants take **carbon dioxide** from the air and turn it into food so they can grow. As they grow, plants also release **oxygen**, which humans need to breathe. Plants help keep the air healthy for people and animals.

Materials

- rubber gloves
- 2 seedlings
- 2 jars with lids
- soil
- water

Steps

1. Wearing the rubber gloves, plant the seedlings in the jars, making sure the roots are covered with soil. Lightly water them.
2. Cover one of the seedlings in more soil, then screw on the lid tightly. Leave the other jar uncovered.
3. Leave both jars in a sunny place for a couple of days. What happens?

105 GOING GREEN

No time for a pet? Grow a plant inside a bottle instead!

WHAT'S THE SCIENCE?

The sun will heat up your greenhouse. Because the lid is sealed, the air inside will stay heated—even when the air outside cools down. The warm air inside can hold more moisture, and as the moisture **condenses** on the greenhouse's cool "roof," it falls on your plants, helping them to grow.

DID YOU KNOW?

Greenhouses must be warm—but not TOO warm, otherwise the plants will cook! Likewise, although they must be humid, greenhouses cannot be too humid or they will promote diseases.

Materials

- clear plastic bottle with lid, washed
- scissors
- soil
- small plant or seedling
- wide sticky tape
- water

Steps

1. Cut the bottle in half (ask an adult to help).
2. Half-fill the bottom part of the bottle with soil. Make sure the soil is slightly moist, and add water if the soil becomes dry during the experiment.
3. Plant the seedling in the soil, making sure you cover all the roots.
4. Tape the top half of the bottle back onto the bottom half, making sure there are no leaks.
5. Put a few drops of water into the bottle then place the lid back on.
6. Place your mini-greenhouse near a window sill where it will get plenty of sun. (Avoid especially dry or sunny places where it might become dry inside the bottle. If unavoidable, monitor the plant for moisture and add small amounts of water if necessary.)

106 HOT STUFF

Which of these cool jars is going to turn into hot stuff?

Materials

* measuring cup
* cold water
* two identical glass jars
* 12 ice cubes
* plastic bag
* thermometer

WHAT'S THE SCIENCE?

Earth's **atmosphere** works just like a greenhouse. When heat from the sun reaches Earth, only some of it escapes back into space. The rest is trapped by Earth's atmosphere. Earth's atmosphere is like a blanket made up of gases, known as **greenhouse gases**. The plastic bag acts just like Earth's atmosphere, trapping the heat.

Steps

1. Put two cups of cold water into each jar, then add six ice cubes to each.
2. Place one of the jars inside the plastic bag, then put both jars outside in direct sunlight.
3. After one hour, check the temperature of the water in each jar.

107 EYE SEE!

Who's the best recycler of them all? Mother Nature, of course!

WHAT'S THE SCIENCE?

Some plants **reproduce** by creating seeds that spread throughout the environment they live in. When a seed lands in good soil, it **germinates** by growing a new root and shoot. Some plants also have "buds," which are shoots that can grow into a new plant on their own. Buds in potatoes are located in the "eye."

Materials

* white potato with "eyes"
* knife
* moist soil
* pot
* water

Steps

1. Cut a 1-in (2.5-cm) chunk from the potato, making sure the piece contains an eye.
2. Add moist soil to the pot, filling it approximately 2 in (5 cm) deep.
3. Plant the chunk of potato inside the soil.
4. Keep the soil moist and watch your potato grow!

108
A-MAZING!

Who knew plants had a sense of direction?!

WHAT'S THE SCIENCE?

Some plants actually grow toward the sun, and will turn their flowers to follow the sun as it moves across the sky throughout the day. This is called **heliotropism**. Sunflowers are famously heliotropic; their flowers turn from east to west as Earth turns each day.

Materials

- dried beans
- soil
- small pot
- water
- large cardboard box with dividers and a lid
- box cutter
- duct tape

Steps

1. Plant your beans in soil inside a small pot. Water the soil.

2. Place the box on its side and cut a hole out of the new top of the box (ask an adult for help). Cut 2–3 in (5–8 cm) holes in the dividers, creating a path for the plant.

3. Put your plant on the bottom of the box and put the lid over the front.

4. Cover any cracks with duct tape.

5. Leave the box in a sunny spot, opening it every few days to water the plant.

6. How long before your plant pokes through the top?

DID YOU KNOW?

A sunflower can grow up to 20 feet tall!

109 OLD MOLD

Mold isn't always ugly—not when it's in a mold rainbow!

WHAT'S THE SCIENCE?

Many **fungi** are decomposers. Decomposers are nature's recyclers because they take dead plants and animals, and recycle them into healthy soil. In this experiment, you can watch as mold breaks up food.

Materials

- food scraps, such as bread, vegetables, fruit, cheese (do not use any meat)
- knife
- chopping board
- water
- clear plastic disposable container, with lid
- tape

Steps

1. Cut the food into 1-in (2.5-cm) pieces, then dip each piece in water.
2. Put the food in the container in a rainbow shape. Make sure the pieces are touching, but don't put them all on top of each other.
3. Put the lid on tightly and seal the container with the tape. Place the container in a place where no one will knock it (or eat it!).
4. Observe the food every day. After a few days you will start to see mold of many different colors. CAREFUL: Don't open the container—many people are allergic to mold.

110 COMPOST QUEEN

Sure, smelly science can be pretty awesome—but you might want to keep a lid on the jar!

WHAT'S THE SCIENCE?

Worms help break down **organic material**, such as food scraps. After they eat the material, they produce special droppings, called **castings**. Worm castings are rich in nutrients, which make our soil healthy.

Materials

- large dark plastic bin with lid, with holes in the lid and the bottom
- old newspapers, slightly damp
- straw, sawdust, shredded leaves
- water
- worms
- food scraps, such as fruit, vegetables, and bread (do not use meat, dairy foods, or eggs)

Steps

1. Set the bin up in the garden, sitting directly on the ground. Fill it with the newspaper, straw, sawdust, and leaves. Make sure the mixture is moist (add a little water if you need to).
2. Put the worms in your compost bin, then add the food scraps.
3. Make sure your compost is slightly moist, but not too wet. Watch it for one month and you will see new soil forming in a thin layer at the bottom of the bin. Over several months you will see this layer of new soil grow. Keep adding shredded newspaper when the worms have eaten the old newspapers.

MY, OH DYE!

Bring an old white T-shirt back to life with the help of a few plants!

WHAT'S THE SCIENCE?

The same pigments that give flowers their colors —carotenoids and anthocyanins—can be used to dye other plant fibers, such as cotton.

Materials

- plant materials (e.g. vegetables, fruits, flower petals, grass, leaves)
- knife
- water
- saucepan
- sieve
- measuring jug
- alum
- plain white T-shirt

DID YOU KNOW?

Some common plants you can use to make dyes are beets/beetroot—red, carrots—yellow, grass—green, raspberries—pink, and coffee—brown.

Steps

1. Chop up your plant materials, then soak them overnight in a water-filled saucepan.
2. Simmer the soggy plant materials for approximately one hour, adding water as needed. (Ask an adult for help.)
3. Using the sieve, strain the dye into a measuring jug and let it cool.
4. Add 1 tablespoon of alum for every 2 pt (945 ml) of dye.
5. Wash your T-shirt with plain detergent. (Do not use fabric softener!)
6. Place the wet T-shirt in the saucepan with the dye and bring it to a simmer (ask an adult for help). When the fabric looks just a bit darker than your desired color, strain the pan over the sink, discarding the dye.
7. Run cold water over the shirt, cooling and rinsing it.
8. Wring the shirt and hang it outdoors to drip dry.

112 BARK MARKS

⚇ ☀ ✂

You get taller as you get older—but trees get wider!

WHAT'S THE SCIENCE?

Every year a tree lives, it forms a growth ring—a layer of new wood. This is called a **cambium**. These rings tell us the age of the tree, but also its history. Thick rings indicate a healthy season with lots of rainfall. Thin rings often indicate a drought.

Materials

- large ball of string
- sticky tape
- scissors
- measuring tape
- pencil and paper

Steps

1. Find a big tree in the backyard or at the park.
2. Tape one end of the string to the tree, then wrap it around the trunk. Cut the string where it meets the end.
3. Measure your piece of string to get the distance around the tree. Record this on your piece of paper.
4. Do this for as many trees as you can find.
5. See which tree has the longest piece of string. Most of the time this is the oldest tree.

113 QUADRANT QUIZ

⚇ ☀ ✂

Get up close and personal with the plants in your own yard!

WHAT'S THE SCIENCE?

Even on a very small scale, different areas of land can be different in many ways—soil, moisture, sunlight, and **acidity** are just a few. These small differences create what are known as **microenvironments**. How many changes can you see in your backyard?

Materials

- yard (meter) ruler
- small sticks
- string
- scissors
- magnifying glass
- notebook
- pencil

Steps

1. In your backyard or at the park, measure a square the length of the ruler. Mark each corner by pushing a stick into the ground.
2. Tie the string to each of the sticks so that it forms a square around the sticks. Look through the magnifying glass and use your notebook to write down what you see, such as the types of plants, the moisture of the soil, and any insects.
3. Make another square in a different part of the yard or park and also record what you see. The types of plants in the squares may differ depending on factors such as the amount of sun, wind and water they receive and nearby animal life.

GREEN

114 MACHINE

Eating salad is healthy—AND smart!

Materials

- different types of edible leaves, such as spinach, lettuce, watercress
- magnifying glass

Steps

1. Examine each of the leaves under a magnifying glass. You will be able to see small lines running through each leaf. These are the veins that carry water through the leaf.

2. Tear the leaves into small pieces and mix together.

3. Serve your leaf salad for dinner!

WHAT'S THE SCIENCE?

As a general fruit and vegetable rule, the darker the color, the healthier it is because it is more packed with **nutrients**. Dark green leafy vegetables are full of **vitamins**, **minerals**, and **antioxidants**. Iron and fiber are two important nutrients in leafy greens, but micronutrients—small chemicals that benefit your body—are found in these as well. Sweet potatoes and broccoli have lots of fiber, vitamin C, and potassium and many berries are high in antioxidants!

POP 'N'

115

STOP

Instead of popping corn, try *growing* some corn!

Materials

- dirt
- plastic zip-lock bag
- water
- popcorn kernels

Steps

1. Put some dirt inside the plastic bag. Add a little water.

2. Put a few popcorn kernels inside the bag and seal it closed.

3. Place the bag on a windowsill with good sunlight.

4. Wait a week, then check it. Do you see any growth?

WHAT'S THE SCIENCE?

A seed contains food that a baby plant will use as it germinates. Because it is usually growing underground, it can't use the sun to spring its first roots and shoots. As soon as the leaf and shoot have uncurled and been exposed to sunlight, the plant begins to use **photosynthesis** to grow.

PAPER PULP

Paper is tough—it can handle being used again and again!

WHAT'S THE SCIENCE?

Paper is made of tough fibers from tree wood that has been shredded and soaked in water, then dried. When paper is soaked in water the fibers come apart again, then when they dry, they stick back together!

DID YOU KNOW?

Recycling paper is important for the planet. It means fewer trees need to be cut down, helps to save energy, and reduces waste.

Materials

- several sheets of paper
- saucepan
- water
- fork
- bowl
- damp cloth
- sieve

Steps

1. Tear the paper into small shreds and put them in the saucepan. Half-fill the saucepan with water.

2. Leave the paper to soak overnight. If all the water has been soaked up by the morning, add a little more.

3. Use the fork to mash the paper into a pulp.

4. Half-fill the bowl with water, then add two handfuls of the pulp. Stir.

5. Place a damp cloth next to the bowl.

6. Use the sieve to scoop the pulp out of the bowl. Hold the sieve over the bowl to drain the water.

7. Tip the pulp out onto the damp cloth, jiggling the sieve to separate the pulp.

8. Press the pulp into an even layer across the cloth, then leave it to dry.

117 HOME NOT-SO-SWEET HOME

Materials

- rubber gloves
- rotting leaves from a compost bin
- plastic funnel
- large clear jar
- aluminum foil
- desk lamp
- magnifying glass

This gives a whole new meaning to the phrase "bugging out!"

Steps

1. Put on the rubber gloves before you start—do not touch the leaves without the gloves.
2. Place the funnel on top of the jar. Loosely place the rotting leaves inside the funnel.
3. Cover the jar with aluminum foil. Ensure the whole jar is covered, to block out all the light.
4. Shine the desk lamp directly onto the jar and leave for about an hour.
5. Now use the magnifying glass to examine the contents of the jar.

WHAT'S THE SCIENCE?

Organic matter, such as rotting leaves, makes a perfect home for smaller organisms that feed on it and also help to break it down. In this experiment, you can use the heat from your lamp to bring bugs that are hiding to light. When the bugs move away from the heat, they fall down the funnel into the jar, where you can see them.

She did it!

Mary Appelhof

A biologist and former high school teacher, "Worm Woman" Mary Appelhof was sure that tons of worms could be eating tons of "garbage." In 1972, Mary made a brochure with an old mimeograph machine, explaining how worms could reduce waste. It was her first attempt at sharing her vision with others. Mary was one of the world's earliest "waste planners," a true visionary in the field of **vermicomposting**. Mary went on to design a "worm bin" called the Worm-a-way®, which is made of recycled plastic and uses a sophisticated ventilation system.

SUPER SPINNER

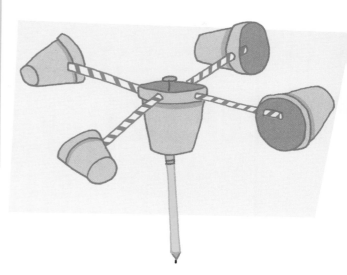

WHAT'S THE SCIENCE?

An **anemometer** is used to measure wind speed. The faster it spins, the faster the wind is blowing. Wind speed is very important to **meteorologists**. They use this information to measure the intensity of hurricanes and to predict the weather.

DID YOU KNOW?

The Saffir-Simpson scale is used to measure the intensity of a hurricane. When winds reach 75 miles per hour (120 km/h), you have a category 1 hurricane. When they reach 155 (250 km/h), it's a category 5—the most severe category there is!

Materials

- 5 Dixie cups/paper cups
- hole punch
- 2 plastic drinking straws
- stapler
- pin
- pencil with an eraser tip

Steps

1. Take one of the Dixie cups/paper cups and punch four holes, evenly spaced, approximately 0.25 in (0.5 cm) below the rim. Punch another hole in the bottom center.

2. Punch a hole in each of the remaining cups, 0.5 in (1.5 cm) below the rim.

3. Push a straw through the hole in one of the four cups, then fold the end of the straw and staple it to the inside of the cup, directly opposite the hole.

4. Repeat step 3 with another of the single-hole cups.

5. Now attach those two cups to the four-hole cup, sliding each straw through two opposite holes, so the straws cross in the center.

6. Attach another one-hole cup to the end of each of the straws. Make sure the cups are all lying on their sides and facing in the same direction around the center cup.

7. Push the pin through the straws where they cross in the center.

8. Push the pencil eraser-first up through the hole in the bottom of the center cup.

9. Push the pin into the eraser. You've made an anemometer!

119 BAROMETER— RIFIC!

Watch the straw—soon you'll be able to predict the weather!

WHAT'S THE SCIENCE?

Barometers are used to measure **air pressure**. Air pressure changes as the weather changes. When the air pressure lowers, this indicates the air is less **dense**. This means that a warmer, low-pressure air mass has moved above your area. These systems often change quickly as the warm air rises. High pressure indicates a dense, colder air mass is above your area. Changes in air pressure often indicate windy or stormy weather is developing.

DID YOU KNOW?

Meteorologists could learn a lot from crickets! Some people claim you can count the number of times they chirp per 15 seconds, add 37, and you will have the current temperature in degrees Fahrenheit!

Materials

- balloon
- scissors
- glass jar
- rubber band
- plastic drinking straw
- tape
- piece of paper
- pen or pencil

Steps

1. Blow up the balloon, then let the air out a couple of times. This will stretch it a bit.
2. Cut the balloon in half, then throw away the end with the "neck."
3. Stretch the remaining half over the top of the jar. Secure it with the rubber band.
4. Lay the straw so that approximately one quarter of it is resting on the jar. Tape the straw loosely in place (not too tight—it needs to be able to move up and down).
5. Tape a piece of paper to the wall and stand the jar in front of it.
6. Mark the level of the straw on the paper.
7. Leave the jar where it is and mark the level every day. Next to each mark note the date and the current weather conditions.

120 TEMP TESTER

Who needs the weather channel? Come up with your own forecasts!

WHAT'S THE SCIENCE?

Scientists use many different instruments to record and predict weather patterns. They may see the temperature dropping, the air pressure rising, and a wind gauge spinning. This could indicate a cold air mass is moving in. Scientists may also see the temperature rising, the air pressure changing, and the wind picking up speed. Sometimes this indicates a storm is on the way.

Materials

- rain gauge (see Experiment #103)
- anemometer (see Experiment #118)
- empty milk crate
- thermometer
- twist tie
- barometer (see Experiment #119)
- paper and pen

Steps

1. Set up your rain gauge and anemometer in an open area near your house or apartment (on a deck or balcony is ideal). Attach them to the milk crate if you like.

2. Attach the thermometer to the inside of the milk crate using the twist tie.

3. Set up your barometer inside.

4. Make a chart with spaces for you to enter the date, time, temperature, rainfall, wind speed, barometer reading, and observations such as cloud cover. Leave a space for a forecast.

5. Observe the weather for two weeks. What sorts of patterns do you notice? Are your forecasts accurate?

121 TORNADO TRAPPER

A tornado can be scary—but not if you're controlling it!

WHAT'S THE SCIENCE?

Tornadoes start with a moist air mass near the ground, swirling horizontally. If a fast cold front, or a cold air mass, comes along, it pulls a column of moist warm air up. This air rises and begins to form a thundercloud at the top, and the winds forming between the warm and cool air whip upwards into a funnel, just like the swirling water in the bottle. The giant cloud on top that caps off the tornado is called the anvil.

Materials

- two 4-pt (2-l) plastic bottles
- water
- duct tape

Steps

1. Pour water into one of the bottles, filling it two-thirds full.

2. Hold the other bottle upside-down over the first bottle. Use duct tape to fasten the two bottles together, spout to spout. Be sure to fasten them tightly so water doesn't spill out!

3. Flip the bottles so the one with the water is on top. Begin swirling the bottle in a circular motion. Watch a "tornado" form as you continue swirling the bottle!

122 SPRAY AWAY

Make your own rivers of color!

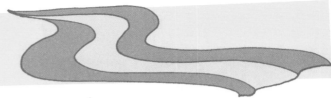

Materials

- sheet of A4 paper
- tape
- sheet of A4 cardboard
- water
- spray bottle
- food coloring

Steps

1. Loosely crumple up the paper.
2. Flatten it out and tape it about 1 in (2.5 cm) in from the edge of the cardboard, so it forms a mountainous-looking region.
3. Put some water in your spray bottle and add the food coloring.
4. Now spray water over the paper. Can you see rivers forming on the paper? Try spraying a little harder.

WHAT'S THE SCIENCE?

Water may be soft but it can also be very powerful. Think about how the water **evaporated** from our oceans falls as rain over mountains and hills. As it runs down the landscape on its way back to the sea, the running water carves the land to form river beds and lakes along the way. These patterns are ages old, and have formed the rivers and lakes around you.

123 MIX IT UP!

Ever wanted to live near the ocean? Make one of your very own!

Materials

- jar
- water
- food coloring
- glitter
- baby oil
- small floating toy

Steps

1. Half-fill the jar with water.
2. Add some food coloring and glitter.
3. Add baby oil until the jar is three-quarters full.
4. Sit a floating toy on top of the oil, then put the lid on the jar.
5. Rock the jar back and forth and watch what happens.

WHAT'S THE SCIENCE?

Water and oil don't mix, because water is denser than oil. As the water in the jar moves, it pushes the oil—causing wave-like shapes. Because it floats, when an oil spill occurs in the ocean, oil can spread out in a wide area over the surface of the water, causing wading birds and marine mammals a lot of harm.

124 LOVELY LAYERS

Who knew you could make a rainbow with just sugar, water, and food coloring!

Materials

- tablespoon
- sugar
- 5 drinking glasses
- water
- red, yellow, green, and blue food coloring

WHAT'S THE SCIENCE?

The sugar solutions made in this experiment vary in **concentration**. The densest solution sits at the bottom and the least dense sits on the top. Density is the amount of matter contained in each unit of volume. It is often measured in grams or milliliters. You can feel differences in density when you swim in a lake, a river, or the sea. Cold water is denser, and you feel it when you dive deeper in the water.

DID YOU KNOW?

Sugar solutions are often miscible—meaning mixable. Eventually the colors in the rainbow cup you create in this experiment will bleed into each other.

Steps

1. Put one tablespoon of sugar into the first glass.
2. Put two tablespoons of sugar into the second glass.
3. Put three tablespoons of sugar into the third glass.
4. Put four tablespoons of sugar into the fourth glass
5. Now stir three tablespoons of water into each glass.
6. Add three drops of red food coloring to the first glass.
7. Add three drops of yellow food coloring to the second glass.
8. Add three drops of green food coloring to the third glass.
9. Add three drops of blue food coloring to the fourth glass.
10. Take the fifth glass and fill it one-quarter full with the blue solution.
11. Slowly and gently spoon some green solution on top of the blue, until the glass is half-full.
12. Fill the glass another quarter of the way with some of the yellow solution.
13. Finally, top it with some of the red solution.

WAY OF THE WIND

125

Windsocks can be decorative and functional!

WHAT'S THE SCIENCE?

Wind changes speed and direction as different air masses change temperature or pressure. Cold air displaces warmer air, and so the wind picks up speed. The rotating Earth affects air masses from polar and **tropical** regions, making wind currents move in patterns over the oceans, mountains and plains. Meteorologists can follow these patterns and try to predict them.

DID YOU KNOW?

Windsocks were first enjoyed hundreds of years ago in Japan. They were flown on "Boys' Day," a holiday celebrating male children. Today, the Japanese celebrate "Children's Day," a holiday for both boys and girls!

Materials

- construction paper
- decorations (stickers, glue, markers, glitter, etc.)
- tape
- scissors
- tissue paper
- glue
- hole punch
- string
- compass

Steps

1. Decorate one side of your piece of paper with stickers, glue, markers, glitter, etc.
2. Roll the paper from one end to the other into a cone shape, with the decorations facing out. Use tape to hold the shape together. Don't make the end too narrow or it will be hard to attach the paper strips in the next step.
3. Cut the tissue paper into long strips. Glue them to the inside bottom of the "windsock."
4. Punch a hole in the top of the windsock. Then punch a second hole on the opposite side.
5. Thread string through the two holes and tie it in a knot.
6. Hang your windsock outside and watch which way the tissue strips blow. Use your compass to determine which direction the wind is coming from.

126 PERFECT PINWHEEL

Decorate your front yard with pinwheels and delight your neighbors!

Materials
- square piece of paper, roughly 9 x 9 in (23 x 23 cm)
- pen
- hole punch
- scissors
- pin
- pencil with eraser tip

Steps
1. Draw a big x across the paper, from corner to corner.
2. Punch a hole in the center of the x.
3. Cut along both lines, stopping approximately 1 in (2.5 cm) from the center hole.
4. Take the top left corner of each corner flap and carefully curve each one in toward the center hole.
5. Secure them in place with the pin.
6. Lay the pencil flat on the table, then push the pin into the side of the eraser.
7. "Plant" your pinwheel in the garden and watch it spin!

WHAT'S THE SCIENCE?

Blades on a pinwheel need to be wide to capture your breath or the wind's motion, and add force to push the blade. **Wind turbines**, however, are exposed to very fast moving winds, and can therefore be thinner and sparser. **Mechanical energy** carried by the wind converts to **electricity** when the blades turn. In a wind turbine this is converted to electricity by an **electromagnet**.

127 WIND WARRIORS

What do you think is blowing in the wind?

Materials
- disposable plastic container lids
- scissors/hole punch
- string
- petroleum jelly

Steps
1. Punch a hole into the top of each lid.
2. Push a piece of string through each hole. Tie a knot at one end so it doesn't slip through the hole. Tie a loop at the other end so you can hang the lids.
3. Cover the top of each lid with petroleum jelly.
4. Hang the lids outside in different places.
5. Collect them after a few hours. What have your lids collected?

WHAT'S THE SCIENCE?

Wind helps distribute many important things in every ecosystem: seeds, **spores**, leaves, sediments—you name it! Wind helps plants to spread their seeds so new plants can grow in different places. Sometimes that species is good for the local environment, and sometimes it isn't. Spores of fungus that ride the wind are great for a forest floor, but not so great inside your home!

128 RIDE THE TIDE

Find out how an earthquake makes Earth move!

Materials

- plastic container on a table
- water
- mallet

Steps

1. Half-fill the container with water.
2. Use the mallet to strike the table on its front edge. This will produce a primary wave.
3. Now strike the top of the table. This will produce a surface wave.
4. Next, strike the side of the table. This will produce a secondary wave.

WHAT'S THE SCIENCE?

Imagine a rock being thrown into water. The waves that move outward are much like the shockwaves caused by an earthquake. Shockwaves vary in type and what they affect. Earthquakes cause three types of waves. Primary waves (or P waves) are the fastest moving. P waves pass through everything—gases, liquids, and solids. Secondary waves (S waves) are a bit slower and only pass through solids. Surface waves (L waves) travel along Earth's surface—they cause the most damage.

129 WATER WATCH

Reduce your water use—stop draining the planet!

Materials

- recent copies of your family's water bills
- paper and markers for reminder signs

Steps

1. Check the bills to see how much water your family uses, then see if you can reduce the amount.
2. Make sure your shower head is a water-efficient model. Ask everyone in your family to take shorter showers.
3. Only run the washing machine and dishwasher when they are full.
4. When you rinse fruits and vegetables, save the water to use on your household plants.
5. Assign each person one water glass each day to cut down on dishes.
6. Ensure everyone turns off the water while brushing their teeth.
7. Review your next water bill. Has your family used less water?

WHAT'S THE SCIENCE?

Did you know that Earth is covered in 72% water? That is an incredible fact, but a little deceiving. 97% of that water is salt water, and not available to drink. Of the remaining 3%, almost 70% is frozen in glaciers and ice caps, and even more is locked in groundwater, wetlands, and other locations. This leaves only 1% of fresh water available for human use. That 1% is constantly cycled through rainfall, clouds, and evaporation. We have to take special care of the water that we use, because it is a limited resource.

130 TISSUE TEST

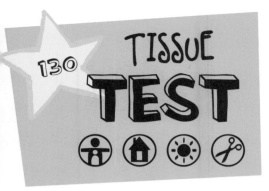

Take a deep breath—does the air taste clean?

Materials

- tissue
- empty jar
- rubber band
- magnifying glass

Steps

1. Lay a damp tissue over the top of the jar. Secure it in place with the rubber band.
2. Leave the jar outside in the open for one day.
3. Bring the jar back inside. Examine the tissue through the magnifying glass. What do you see? You may discover natural items, such as pollen from flowers. You also might find artificial items, such as particles of soot.

WHAT'S THE SCIENCE?

Air pollution is a big problem, caused by particles in the air that can damage soil, dissolve in water, and harm human health. Air particles, or particulate matter, is counted by scientists in "parts per million." Even small amounts of pollution can cause damage—that's why such precise and tiny measurements are used! Small particles come from cars, factories, fires, manufacturing chemicals, burning coal, and much more. The average adult breathes over 3000 gallons (11 356 L) of air every day, so clearing our air is important for everyone.

131 POLLUTION PATROL

Losing your bounce? Could be pollution!

Materials

- 2 metal coat hangers
- 8 rubber bands
- plastic bag
- tape
- magnifying glass

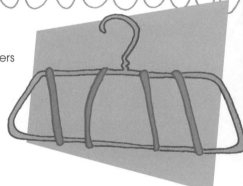

Steps

1. Bend each coat hanger into a rectangle.
2. Put four rubber bands around each rectangle, stretching them tight.
3. Hang one of the rectangles outside in a shady spot.
4. Place the other rectangle inside the plastic bag. Tape the bag tightly shut and put the sealed bag inside a drawer.
5. Examine the rubber bands after a week. Check how well they stretch.
6. Keep checking them once a week. If you live in a polluted area, the rubber bands left outside will break into pieces after a few weeks. In clean air, however, they will stay intact for much longer.

WHAT'S THE SCIENCE?

Pollutants such as **ozone** and acid in the air cause rubber to degrade, or lose its stretchy properties. Rubber **molecules** are shaped like very long chains. Pollutants create cracks in these chains, causing the bands to break.

132 RAIN PAIN

Materials

- vinegar
- 3 identical jars
- water
- labels and markers
- 3 identical plants

Rain, rain, go away, come again another day—unless you're acid rain!

WHAT'S THE SCIENCE?

When some products (such as paper) are manufactured, gases are released into the air. These gases can dissolve into rain as it falls to Earth. Rain containing these pollutants is called acid rain. Even mildly acidic rain can break down rocks, add acid to soil, and cause oceans to acidify. This causes problems for many living things.

Steps

1. Pour vinegar into one of the jars, filling it one quarter full. Then fill the jar to the top with water. Label this jar "low acid."
2. Half-fill the second jar with vinegar, then fill the jar with water. Label this jar "high acid."
3. Fill the third jar completely with water. Label this jar "water."
4. Place one plant next to each jar.
5. For a couple of weeks, water each plant with the solution in its partner jar. What happens to the plants?

133 MINERALS CALLING!

Learn about **toxic** electronics, and help the Earth!

WHAT'S THE SCIENCE?

Some electronic items contain toxic metals and minerals. When **electronic waste** goes into **landfill**, these substances leach out and harm the environment. Some of the metals and minerals in these items, such as lead, cadmium, aluminum, copper, and gold, can be recovered and recycled.

Materials

- computer and Internet access
- piece of poster board
- markers
- decorations and magazine pictures of electronics
- cardboard box
- scissors and glue

Steps

1. Jump online and find out who is collecting electronic waste in your area.
2. Make a poster that explains what electronic waste is—educate your friends and family! Include facts about recycling metals and the toxic properties of lead and other computer parts.
3. Design a box for people to deposit their old phones, cameras, and small electronic appliances. Decorate the box, and make a sign explaining what it is for.
4. Place your box in a prominent place, such as near the recycling center, or near the front door. If your school is able to partner with a collection program, the school could raise money by collecting phones and selling them to recyclers.

134 WILD WETLANDS

Wetlands are working all kinds of magic—find out how!

WHAT'S THE SCIENCE?

Wetlands are unique swampy environments. When it rains on an ecosystem with wetlands, the shape of the land slows the water flow and redirects it to low-lying areas around rivers or streams. Sediments and plants help filter the water before it flows back into rivers, providing wildlife with healthy water.

Materials

- three plastic cups
- flat tray
- friend
- two pitchers/jugs of water
- handful of gravel or small rocks
- 1.7 fl oz (50 ml) coffee

Steps

1. Place one plastic cup on a tray. Poke small holes in the bottom of the second cup. Sit it next to the first.

2. With a friend, pour water into the cups until they are overflowing. See how the water flows out of each cup differently.

3. Poke small holes in the bottom of the third cup. Fill it with gravel. Combine two cups of water and coffee in a pitcher.

4. Slowly pour the coffee mixture over the rocks. Look at the water as it runs into the tray. Has the color changed?

135 SUN JUICE

Who wouldn't want a jar of sunlight?!

WHAT'S THE SCIENCE?

Solar panels convert sunlight into electricity. The electricity can then be stored in batteries so it can be used later.

DID YOU KNOW?

The International Space Station (ISS) uses solar panels to generate power.

Materials

- newspaper
- duct tape
- glass jelly (jam) jar
- glass frosting spray
- solar garden light
- hot glue gun

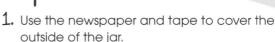

Steps

1. Use the newspaper and tape to cover the outside of the jar.

2. Spray a light coat of frosting spray on the inside of the jar.

3. Ask an adult to help you to separate the solar light unit from the bulb and stake that it came with.

4. Ask an adult to help you use the hot glue gun to attach the solar light unit to the inside of the jar's lid.

5. Take the newspaper off the jar.

6. Keep your jar in direct sunlight during the day—and watch it shine!

136 SUN SNACKS

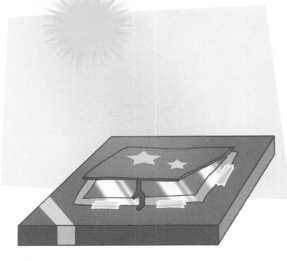

Harness the sun's energy—and enjoy a toasty treat!

WHAT'S THE SCIENCE?

Solar ovens work by using a reflector—in this case the aluminum foil—to gather and concentrate the sun's rays.

DID YOU KNOW?

Scientists can concentrate sunlight up to 60,000 times!

Materials

- large sheet of notebook paper
- empty pizza box
- marker
- scissors
- tape
- aluminum foil
- black construction paper
- plastic wrap
- snack you want to heat up
- small stick

Steps

1. Put the notebook paper on top of the pizza box lid, in the center. Trace its outline.
2. Cut along three sides of the outline, then fold along the fourth, forming a cardboard flap.
3. Tape a piece of aluminum foil over the inside of the flap.
4. Open the box. Line the bottom with the construction paper.
5. Cut two pieces of plastic wrap, about 1 in (2.5 cm) larger than the flap opening.
6. Tape one plastic piece over the inside of the opening, and the other piece on the outside.
7. Place your snack in the center of the box, then close the lid and open the flap.
8. Place the box in direct sunlight and prop open the flap with a stick.
9. Wait 30 minutes, then check on your snack. Is it warm?

137 SPILL SAVER

Cleaning up after an oil spill is tough—
but important—work!

Materials

- 3.4 fl oz (100 ml) vegetable oil
- 1 pt (500 ml) of water in a shallow bowl
- spoon
- plastic drinking straw
- handful of grass or straw
- 4-in (10-cm) piece of string

Steps

1. Pour the oil into the water.
2. Use your tools to try to re-collect the oil. Measure how much you can recover.

WHAT'S THE SCIENCE?

Instead of mixing with water, oil breaks up into very small amounts that are hard to remove. The objects used in this experiment are very similar to real oil spill recovery tools. The string is like a "boom" that is used to stop the oil from spreading. The straw can be used to "vacuum" oil. The spoon is like the large mechanical scoops used to collect oil from the surface. Straw and grass are sometimes used to absorb oil. Scientists also use **bacteria**, **chemical dispersants**, and machines to collect oil.

138 WATER WARMER

Solar power is hot stuff!

Materials

- cold water
- baking tray (if it is not a dark color, cover it in black plastic)
- thermometer
- clear plastic sheet

Steps

1. Pour the cold water into the baking tray, filling it 0.5 in (1 cm) deep.
2. Use your thermometer to check the temperature of the water.
3. Position the plastic sheet over the tray and leave it in direct sunlight for one hour.
4. Remove the plastic sheet from the tray and check the temperature of the water again. How has it changed?

WHAT'S THE SCIENCE?

When sunlight hits a surface, its light energy is converted into heat energy. The black tray is opaque and absorbs heat, because black material can absorb all the **frequencies** of light in sunlight. The clear plastic allows some of the light to pass through, and **reflects** a small amount of light too. Therefore, it does not absorb as much heat.

139 ★ ROOF REFLECTIONS

The color of your roof could be heating up your house!

WHAT'S THE SCIENCE?

Some colors reflect light and others absorb it. Places on Earth with a lot of ice, for example, are mostly white and reflect light—staying cool. Places that are darker, such as surfaces covered in soil, absorb light—and therefore, collect heat. The "albedo" of a surface refers to how much sunlight it reflects.

Materials

- 2 pieces of white construction paper
- 2 pieces of black construction paper
- 2 thermometers
- 1 timer

Steps

1. Construct two paper houses using the illustration on this page as a guide. Make one house all black and one all white.
2. Place a thermometer in each house and measure the temperature.
3. Check the temperature every 30 minutes for a few hours. How does it change?

She did it!

Maria Telkes

Hungarian-born Maria Telkes first became interested in solar power as a high school student. After high school, she went on to become a doctor of **physical chemistry**, before moving to the United States in 1925. In 1948, she worked with a team (including many other women!) on an experimental house designed to demonstrate the uses of solar energy. Maria was in charge of designing its heating system. The house is still in use today. Maria went on to develop several other uses of solar energy and won awards for her research.

140 PLASTIC PLANTERS

Turn your empty soft drink bottles into plant paradise!

WHAT'S THE SCIENCE?

How much water does your plant need? It will often give you tell-tale signs that it has too much or too little. Plants that wilt have too little water, and need to be watered more evenly. Some plants can become overwatered—they will have moldy roots, yellow leaves, or soft, mushy stems.

Materials

- 1 large plastic soft drink bottle
- scissors
- small piece of gauze or loose cloth
- rubber band
- potting mix
- seedling
- water
- cup or container

Steps

1. Cut off the top third of your soda bottle. Keep the top and recycle the rest of the bottle.
2. Hold the bottle top upside down and cover the spout with the gauze, fixing it into place with a rubber band.
3. Fill the bottle top with potting mix, leaving a small gap at the top. Plant your seedling in the soil.
4. Add enough water to make the soil moist, but not wet. Remove the gauze from the neck after the seedling has been planted and sit the planter in a cup or container. The bottle can be lifted out and examined to see roots growing out of the neck!

141 SWEET TWEETS

When you encourage birds to live around your house or apartment, you are supporting habitat health. You also get a chance to learn about the **biodiversity** of your area by observing the birds that visit your feeder!

WHAT'S THE SCIENCE?

There are over 10 000 species of birds in the world! Your local ecosystem may support many species. With a little research, you can find out what common birds are in your area and what their healthiest food choices are. The bird feeder below can be filled with whatever food your local **ecologist** or park ranger recommends.

Materials

- scissors
- soda bottle
- wooden spoons
- small eye screw
- rope or twine

Steps

1. Cut two pairs of opposing holes in your bottle about 1/2 way and 1/3 of the way from the bottom so that you can slide your dowel through the bottle and have two ends sticking out. Slide the dowels through.
2. Fill the bottle with bird food appropriate for your neighborhood.
3. Twist a small eye screw into the bottle top so that you can hang it from a tree or other location. Replace the bottle cap.
4. Keep a journal of the birds that visit, and get a bird guide so that you can learn their species names!

142 GOING GLOBAL

Did you know you that you practically have the entire world in your kitchen?

WHAT'S THE SCIENCE?

Many of the ingredients in the foods you eat come from other continents around the world. That is because different crops grow best in different climates, and different animals live in different environments. Your kitchen is a wonderful example of biodiversity in the food we eat.

Materials

- markers
- poster board
- star stickers

Steps

1. Copy the world map on this page or from an atlas or map onto the poster board.
2. Explore your kitchen. Check packaging details to see where the items in your cupboards and refrigerator come from. Add them to your world map.

143 TRASH TALK

Let's talk trash—but not the gross kind! The kind our planet loves!

WHAT'S THE SCIENCE?

Some materials are **biodegradable**. Biodegradable materials can help Earth, fertilizing soil and nourishing plants as they break down. Most items that occur naturally on Earth—such as apple cores and orange peels—are biodegradable. Materials made by humans are not usually biodegradable. Non-biodegradable materials go into landfill and can pollute Earth.

Materials

- dirt
- empty milk carton
- lettuce
- small plastic bag
- cup of water
- stick

Steps

1. Pour dirt into the milk carton, filling it halfway.
2. Put the lettuce and plastic bag on top of the dirt.
3. Pour the water on top of the lettuce and plastic.
4. Check back on the milk carton a week later. Poke it with the stick to find your trash. Which decomposed faster, the lettuce or the plastic?

WONDER WORDS

acidity—A measure of how "acidic" a substance is. This depends on the number of hydrogen ions present in the substance.

aerate—To expose to or infuse with air.

air pressure—The weight of the air above you puts pressure on you, and on the entire surface of Earth. Meteorologists measure this pressure in Newtons or pounds per square inch.

anemometer—An instrument used to measure wind force and velocity.

antioxidants—Chemical substances that protect body cells from the harmful effects of oxidation (the chemical combination of a substance with an oxidizing agent).

atmosphere—The mixture of gases that surrounds celestial bodies, such as planets.

bacteria—Microscopic, single-celled organisms that are capable of causing disease.

barometers—Instruments used by meteorologists for measuring atmospheric pressure.

biodegradable—Capable of being broken down into harmless by-products by living things, such as bacteria.

biodiversity—The variety of living organisms, including plants, animals, and micro-organisms, in an ecosystem.

cambium—The layer of living cells under the bark of a tree where the growth ring forms.

carbon dioxide—A colorless gas, containing one carbon atom and two oxygen atoms. It plays an important role in many chemical reactions, such as photosynthesis and cellular respiration. It also makes up a small part of Earth's atmosphere.

castings—Earthworm droppings that can be used as fertilizer.

chemical dispersants—Chemicals that, when added to oil, help break it up. These are used in oil spills and dishwashing soap. They contain surfactants.

concentration—The amount of substance that is dissolved in a liquid is referred to as its concentration. If you have a strong saline concentration, that means a lot of salt has been dissolved in water.

condenses—Changes into a form that is more concentrated and less dense, forming condensation.

decompose—The process by which something breaks down into simpler compounds, or decays.

dense—Tightly packed with molecules.

distilling—Purifying a liquid by evaporating it and then collecting its condensation.

ecosystem—A group of animals, birds, fish, people, microorganisms, soil, and water that coexist in a specific area.

ecologist—Scientist who studies the relationship between living things and their environment.

electricity—The flow of an electron charge, often in a current. Electricity can occur in many forms, such as static electricity or lightning.

electromagnet—A magnet whose core is made of insulated wire wrapped around soft iron, which becomes magnetized when currents pass through the wire.

electronic waste—Computers, televisions, old phones, and many other electronic devices make up electronic waste. Electronic waste contains both valuable and toxic metals, so needs to be recycled and disposed of responsibly.

erodes—Wears away or destroys.

evaporating—Changing from a liquid into a gas.

extract—To draw out, either chemically or physically.

frequencies—Measures of how often a wave "vibrates" in a given amount of time. For example, light waves travel in Hz, or waves per second.

fungi—Fungi make up their own kingdom of living things. They don't contain chlorophyll and they feed on organic matter.

germinates—Causes to grow or sprout.

greenhouse gases—Gases in Earth's atmosphere that affect the temperature of Earth by trapping heat.

habitats—Environments that are home to particular plants, animals, or other living things.

heliotropism—When plants grow or move towards the angle of the sun.

landfill—A trash disposal system in which waste is buried between layers of Earth.

mechanical energy—The sum of potential energy and kinetic energy in a machine or system.

meteorologists—Scientists who study the atmosphere and forecast weather conditions.

microenvironments—Small areas where factors like humidity, soil, or acidity produce an environment that encourages the growth of specific small living things and even micro-organisms.

minerals—Minerals are substances formed in Earth's crust that have a regular chemical composition and recognizable physical properties. Some minerals are made up of one element, others of many molecules.

molecules—Several atoms bonded together.

nutrients—Sources of materials essential for an organism to be healthy.

organic material—Animal or plant material.

organisms—Living things.

oxygen—A colorless, odorless, tasteless gas that makes up about one-fifth of Earth's atmosphere and can be found in water and most rocks and minerals.

ozone—A gas found in Earth's stratosphere. Ozone blocks ultraviolet radiation from the sun.

photosynthesis—How plants use the sun's energy to convert carbon dioxide and water into food.

physical chemistry—The branch of chemistry concerned with the molecular and atomic levels of how materials behave and how chemical reactions occur.

pigments—Substances that mix with other materials to give them color.

polar—Polar refers to the regions above and below 60 degrees latitude in the north and south ends of Earth.

pollutants—Impurities that contaminate environments.

pores—Tiny openings in skin (for perspiration or water absorption) or a leaf (for gas exchange of carbon dioxide and oxygen and for releasing water vapor).

reflects—Bounces back light, heat, or sound waves from a surface.

reproduce—Produce offspring or young.

sediments—Materials that have been broken down by weathering and erosion.

spores—Small cells made by plants that can grow into new organisms. Spores function in some ways like seeds.

toxic—Describes something that can damage an organism by using a toxin (poison).

tropical—The region of Earth surrounding the equator, or places with climates similar to that region.

vermicomposting—Using worms to process organic waste and convert it into natural fertilizer.

vitamins—Substances that, in small quantities, are essential to the nutrition of animals and plants.

wetland—Land that has moist soil or is covered in shallow water.

wind turbine—Windmills that capture the wind's energy to make their blades turn a magnet within a wire, and create an electromagnetic current that can be used to add power to a region's grid.

NIGHT OWL
ASTONOMY

144 MARVELOUS MOBILE

This is one experiment where you can totally space out!

WHAT'S THE SCIENCE?

Our solar system, which formed more than 4.5 billion years ago, consists of **asteroids**, **comets**, **moons**, and **planets**. All of the objects in our solar system **orbit** around the **sun**. They are pulled by its strong **gravity**. That's why the sun is known as a "parent **star**."

Materials

- newspaper
- bucket of water
- papier mâché glue
- paints
- 5 to 6 ft (1.5 to 2 m) of wire
- needle or skewer
- 2 bamboo sticks
- torch
- one 1 in (2.5 cm) styrofoam ball (for Earth's moon)

- three 2 in (5 cm) styrofoam balls (for Mercury, Mars and Pluto)
- four 3 in (7.5 cm) styrofoam balls (for Venus, Earth, Uranus and Neptune)
- two 4 in (10 cm) styrofoam balls (for Jupiter and Saturn)
- one 8 in (20 cm) styrofoam ball (for the sun)

Steps

1. Tear the newspaper into pieces and leave them overnight to soak in a bucket of water.
2. The next day, squeeze the water out of the newspaper.
3. Make the newspaper into planets by dipping it into the glue and molding it over each of the styrofoam balls. You will need to make eight planets, plus the sun, Earth's moon and Pluto (which used to be classified as a planet but was reclassified as a **dwarf planet** in 2006).
4. Leave your planets to dry.
5. Paint your planets in their different colors.
6. Bend some of the wire into star shapes to hang next to your planets.
7. Push the needle through each planet, then thread a length of wire through each hole.
8. Place one bamboo stick across the other to form a cross shape. Attach another piece of wire and make a loop so that you can hang your mobile up.
9. Hang your planets and stars from the two bamboo sticks using the wire.
10. Turn the lights off and shine a torch onto your solar system.

SUN

MERCURY

VENUS

EARTH

EARTH'S MOON

MARS

JUPITER

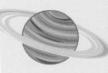

SATURN

URANUS

NEPTUNE

PLUTO

DID YOU KNOW?

Many people use this mnemonic device to remember the order of the planets in relation to the sun: My Very Energetic Mother Just Served Us Noodles!

145 ROCKING OUT

Ever wonder how far away the stars in the sky really are?

WHAT'S THE SCIENCE?

Even though you haven't moved, the pencil appears to have shifted because your line of sight has changed. **Astronomers** take this into account when measuring the distance to nearby stars. This is called measuring their **parallax**. They know that the stars will appear to be different distances from Earth depending on where they are measured from. To account for this, one way to make accurate measurements of stars from Earth is to take the measurements six months apart—when Earth moves from one side of the sun to the other. The parallax occurs in the middle of the two points.

Materials

- bookshelf
- pencil

Steps

1. Stand in front of a bookshelf and hold your pencil in front of you as far as your arm will stretch. Focus your eyes on the bookshelf.
2. Close your left eye and make a note of where you see the pencil against the bookshelf.
3. Without changing position at all, open your left eye and close your right eye instead.
4. What do you notice about the position of the pencil?

She did it!

Henrietta Leavitt

American-born Henrietta Leavitt discovered astronomy as a senior in high school. After she graduated from college she began volunteering as a research assistant at the Harvard College Observatory. Seven years later she was employed at the observatory—earning US 30 cents an hour! Henrietta studied images of stars in order to determine their **magnitude**. She eventually became head of the photographic **photometry** department. Over the course of her career, Henrietta discovered more than 2400 stars.

146 GET FOCUSED

Get up close and personal with space!

WHAT'S THE SCIENCE?

Telescopes use two different **lenses** to collect light from far-away objects. The large lens, or objective lens, focuses the light. The eyepiece, or the lower-powered lens, magnifies the image so that you can see it.

Materials

- tape
- large lens (such as the lens from an old pair of reading glasses or the lens from a big toy magnifying glass)
- two paper tubes about 15 in (40 cm) long. One should be able to slide in and out of the other.
- smaller lens (such as the lens from a mini magnifying glass)

Steps

1. Tape the large lens to the end of the wider tube.
2. Tape the smaller lens to the end of the smaller tube.
3. Slide the smaller tube into the larger one so there is one lens on each end. You have created a simple **refracting** telescope! Try it out! Does your telescope help you to see distant objects more clearly?

147 FRUIT FALL

It's a race between the orange and the grape!

WHAT'S THE SCIENCE?

The force on Earth that pulls everything down and stops it from floating away is called gravity. No matter how much an object weighs, gravity pulls it downward at the same speed.

Materials

- newspaper
- chair
- 2 oranges
- grape

Steps

1. Spread the newspaper out on the floor then place the chair on top of it.
2. Carefully stand on the chair.
3. Hold one orange in each hand, extending your arms out in front. Make sure each orange is at the same height.
4. Drop the oranges at the same time. Which lands first?
5. Try it again, this time with an orange and a grape. Which one lands first?

148 DON'T SPILL

Don't let gravity get you down!

WHAT'S THE SCIENCE?

Gravity is a force that dictates the way objects interact, including moons, planets, and stars. The larger an object is, the stronger its gravity is. Gravity is hard to measure using small objects. The marbles are quite small, so they do not exert a strong gravitational pull on each other. However, they DO experience a gravitational pull toward Earth, which is *much* larger!

Materials

- plastic wrap or garbage bags
- embroidery hoop
- two piles of books or bricks
- marbles

Steps

1. Stretch the plastic wrap or garbage bag inside the embroidery hoop. Secure it in place with the outer hoop, ensuring it is stretched tight.
2. Place the hoop between your books or bricks so it is resting on top of them.
3. Consider the plastic sheet "space." Put a marble on it. What happens?
4. Add another marble to the plastic sheet. Now what happens?

149 POP TOP

Find out which materials are best suited to outer space!

Materials

- balloon
- scissors
- empty soft drink can
- hot water
- fat rubber band

Steps

1. Cut the neck off your balloon.
2. Twist the pop top (or pull tab) off the can, then pour hot water into it. (Ask an adult to help you.)
3. Stretch the balloon over the top of the can and secure it with the rubber band.
4. Record what happens first with the hot water, then as the water cools, and finally when the water is cold.

WHAT'S THE SCIENCE?

The temperature in space—beyond Earth's atmosphere—can be very cold, but **solar radiation** shines on everything. Some materials may change shape depending on the way they **absorb** or **reflect** light. The clothes you wear at home would not give your body the protection it needs in space. At the International Space Station (where **astronauts** live and work), the radiation from the sun is high because the radiation isn't filtered through an **atmosphere**, as it is on Earth.

150 GRAVITY GOTCHA

Feeling a bit unbalanced?
This could be why!

WHAT'S THE SCIENCE?

The center of gravity is the point where all of the **matter** is balanced out, or at an average. If two objects are the same mass, their center is the mid-point between them. If one is larger, the center is closer to the larger object. When you jump, you shift your center of gravity. When your hands are under your toes, you cannot shift your center of gravity forward!

Materials
- you!

Steps

1. Stand with your feet hip-width apart.
2. Bend over and swing your hands near your toes.
3. Jump forward.
4. Now put your hands, gently, under your toes.
5. Try to jump forward now. What happens?

151 UP FRONT AND CENTER

See if you can find the perfect balance point!

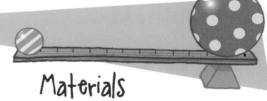

Materials
- long ruler
- triangular block
- small, light objects or toys that can balance on a ruler

Steps

1. Balance the ruler on your triangular block. The triangle should be in the middle, acting as a fulcrum.
2. Choose two objects and place them on either end of the ruler. See where you need to move the fulcrum in order to balance the masses of the two objects.
3. Try changing objects to see where the new balance point will be.

WHAT'S THE SCIENCE?

The center of gravity between two planets will be closer to the larger planet. If you place a larger object on your ruler, you need to move the **fulcrum**, which represents the center of gravity, toward it, to balance it out. It's like a see-saw—the center of gravity is the point where the board balances. If the children at each end of the see saw are the same size, the balance is equal. If one child is bigger, the smaller child must apply more force to create balance.

152 DAY AND NIGHT!

Just as you're waking up, kids on the other side of the world are hitting their pillows!

WHAT'S THE SCIENCE?

Earth is like a giant ball in the darkness of space. Earth is always moving and spinning on its **axis**, which is tilted at an angle of 23 degrees. It takes around 24 hours to do one complete spin. When one side of Earth is facing the sun, the people in that part of Earth experience daytime, while on the other side it is nighttime.

Materials

- paper and pen
- scissors
- sticky tape
- inflated balloon
- atlas
- piece of string
- flashlight/torch

Steps

1. Draw the shapes of the different continents on the paper. Cut them out and tape them onto the balloon in their correct positions. (Use an atlas if you need help.)
2. Use the string to hang the balloon somewhere.
3. Shine the flashlight/torch onto one side of the balloon. This represents the sun.
4. Slowly turn the balloon.
5. Try turning the balloon to show these times in different parts of the world: midnight, sunrise, midday, sunset.

DID YOU KNOW?

Earth turns to the east as it rotates. This is why the sun rises in the east—as we spin around to face it!

153 SHAPE UP!

Would you have ever guessed that Earth is slightly squashed?

WHAT'S THE SCIENCE?

Earth is round, but it is not a perfect sphere. It is actually an oblate spheroid, which means it is flattened slightly at its **poles**. Earth's "squashed" shape is a result of its **rotation**. It bulges out at the **equator** as it spins. The Earth rotates on an axis, the ends of which are at the poles.

Materials

- balloon
- water
- hand drill
- screw eye (screw with a loop on one end)
- string

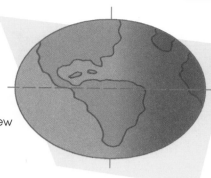

Steps

1. Fill the balloon with water and tie the neck closed.
2. Put a screw eye into your hand drill where the drill bit normally goes. (Ask an adult for help.)
3. Tie the piece of string to the screw eye. Tie the other end of the string to the balloon.
4. Go outside or to a sink and start to turn the handle of the drill.
5. Gradually add more speed.

154 DIALED IN

What time is it? Time to learn about sundials, of course!

WHAT'S THE SCIENCE?

Long ago, before clocks were invented, people used sundials to work out what time it was. They did this by studying the position of the sun in the sky and the length of the shadows cast by vertical sticks.

Materials

- pencil
- rocks
- marker

Steps

1. Find a sunny place outside, with no shade.
2. Stick the pencil in the ground.
3. Watch the shadow cast by the pencil throughout the day. Each hour, put a rock where the shadow is cast. Use the marker to write the time on each rock. You will slowly create a ring of rocks.
4. Try telling the time using just your rocks, then check a clock or watch to see if you were right. Can you tell the time within 15 minute intervals by looking at the shadows between the rocks?

155

TIDE GUIDE

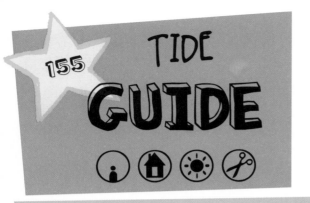

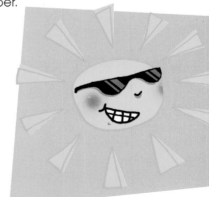

SURF'S UP!

Materials

- bucket
- water
- plastic ball

Just like your days have ups and downs, the ocean has high and low tides!

WHAT'S THE SCIENCE?

Seventy percent of Earth's surface is covered with oceans. Every 12 hours the tides rise and fall. This happens without the level of water changing. As Earth and the moon spin, gravity pulls them together and the moon pulls at the ocean water directly beneath it, causing it to rise and fall. When it is high tide on one side of Earth, it will be low tide on the other side.

Steps

1. Half fill the bucket with water.
2. Float the ball in the bucket.
3. Using both hands, push the ball down very slowly.
4. Let the ball come up again.
5. Watch the change in water level.

156

RAY PLAY

Materials

- sheet of paper
- drinking glass
- water

Steps

1. Find a sunny spot.
2. Place the sheet of paper on a flat surface.
3. Half fill the glass with water.
4. Hold the glass about 3 in (8 cm) above the sheet of paper.
5. Slowly move the glass up and down, and tilt it on a slight angle.
6. Note any colors that you see on the paper.

The sun's rays make us feel nice and warm— but they are also quite informative!

WHAT'S THE SCIENCE?

Light from the sun (and any other star) can be broken down into many colors, or **frequencies**. These frequencies tell astronomers what **elements** are present in each star. We know that the sun is basically a big ball of gas and **plasma**. Most of its gas is made up of helium or hydrogen. But its light bands tell us that it also contains oxygen, carbon, iron, magnesium, and nitrogen.

157 SUN FUN

Every day is a chance to see something a little differently ...

WHAT'S THE SCIENCE?

As the sun moves between dawn and dusk it reaches an **apex**, or high point, at noon each day. If you live near the equator, the sun takes about 12 hours to go from east to west. If you live further from the equator, the place where the sun rises and sets, as well as the apex, changes with the seasons. In the winter, the sun is low in the sky, and the days are shorter. In the summer, the sun is high in the sky and we get long summer days.

Materials

- compass
- sunglasses
- pen and paper

Steps

1. Go outdoors. Make sure you are facing either east or west (check the compass), then find a nearby tree and a far-away object.

2. Stand so that the tree and the far-away object are in line. This will help you make sure you are always looking at the same spot.

3. At dawn or dusk each day, take note of where the sun appears in relation to your object. Wear sunglasses so you don't hurt your eyes.

4. Record the sun's position daily for 1–2 weeks. You should start to see some changes.

---

158 SUN SAFE

NEVER stare directly at the sun— you'll fry your eyes!

WHAT'S THE SCIENCE?

The spots you see on the piece of cardboard are sunspots—dark spots that appear on the surface of the sun. They are magnetic spots that are much cooler than the gas around them. These sunspots come and go fairly regularly. They increase and decrease in intensity in periods of around 11 years, although this can vary. This cycle is called the "Sunspot Cycle."

Materials

- sharp pencil
- 2 pieces of cardboard

Steps

1. Using the sharp pencil, make a small hole in one of the pieces of cardboard.

2. Go outside and stand with your back to the sun.

3. Hold up the card with the hole in it.

4. Hold the other piece of card about 8 in (20 cm) below it, so that the sun shines through the hole in the first card onto the lower piece.

5. Observe what is happening.

6. Move the card pieces further apart.

7. Observe what is happening.

159 SUNSET IN A BOX

Tell your mom and dad you are on a dusting strike—in the name of scientific discovery!

Materials

- clear plastic box
- water
- 1 teaspoon milk
- flashlight/torch

Steps

1. Fill the plastic box with water.
2. Add the milk to the water.
3. Shine a torch straight down onto the water. This is what the sun looks like at midday.
4. Now shine the torch sideways to see what the sun looks like as it sets.

WHAT'S THE SCIENCE?

Earth's atmosphere is full of dust particles. The particles scatter light as it travels to Earth. Different colors of light have different **wavelengths**. Shorter wavelengths are more easily scattered. When the sun is low on the horizon the light waves have further to travel to reach our eyes. Red and yellow light waves are longer than other colors, which is why we see them during a sunset—they are the only ones not scattered.

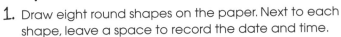

160 MOON MONITOR

How many faces does the moon really have?

WHAT'S THE SCIENCE?

The moon **revolves** around Earth. We can see the moon because it is reflecting light from the sun. As the moon revolves around Earth it also rotates slowly on its axis. This changes the amount of light it reflects, which is what makes it appear to be changing shape.

Materials

- pencil
- paper
- clipboard
- clock

Steps

1. Draw eight round shapes on the paper. Next to each shape, leave a space to record the date and time.
2. On a clear night, go outside and observe the shape of the moon. Color the first shape on your paper to look like the moon in the sky. Note the date and time next to it.
3. Wait two nights then observe the shape of the moon again. Color the second circle.
4. Do this every second night until each of the eight shapes is completed.

161 MOON MAGIC

Just as people have many moods, the moon has many phases!

WHAT'S THE SCIENCE?

The moon passes through eight phases each month. The phases are named after how much of the moon we can see, and whether or not it is increasing or diminishing in size. They are:
NEW MOON
WAXING CRESCENT
FIRST QUARTER
WAXING GIBBOUS
FULL MOON
WANING GIBBOUS
LAST QUARTER
WANING CRESCENT

DID YOU KNOW?

The moon spins as it orbits Earth, which means the same side is always facing Earth. The other side remained a mystery until the Russian space probe Luna 3 explored it in 1956. The pictures the probe sent back showed that the other side had even more **craters** *than the side we can see!*

Materials

- shoebox
- black paint
- scissors or stanley knife (ask an adult for help)
- flashlight/torch
- tape
- ping pong ball

Steps

1. Paint the inside of the shoebox black.
2. Using the scissors or knife, cut three holes, evenly spaced, along each side of the shoebox. Make the holes about 0.25 in (7 mm) across.
3. Cut another hole of the same size at one end of the shoebox.
4. At the other end cut a hole big enough for the flashlight/torch to shine through.
5. Using tape, suspend the ping pong ball in the center of the shoebox. It should be at the same height as the holes you have cut in the sides of the shoebox.
6. Hold the torch in place and turn it on.
7. Look into each hole. Can you see the phases of the moon?

NORTHERN   SOUTHERN

NEW

WAXING CRESCENT

FIRST QUARTER

WAXING GIBBOUS

FULL

WANING GIBBOUS

LAST QUARTER

WANING CRESCENT

In the northern hemisphere the light part of the moon moves right to left: in the southern hemisphere it moves left to right. With support, lean over and look at the moon with your head upside down; that's how the other hemisphere sees it!

162 MOON ROCKS

Rock out with some moon rocks tonight!

WHAT'S THE SCIENCE?

The moon is covered in mountains, valleys, and holes called craters. Most of the moon's surface is made up of **regolith**. Regolith is a loose layer of broken rocks, dust, and soil. Many **moon rocks** are breccias. Breccias are hard rocks that were once broken apart—possibly by **meteors**—but re-formed. Astronomers have also found a **dense**, hard rock on the moon called basalt, which we have here on Earth, too!

Materials

- ball of clay or play dough
- hot water
- old tennis ball
- pencil

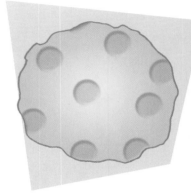

Steps

1. Roll the ball of clay or play dough in hot water. Leave it somewhere warm for 15 minutes.
2. Cover the outside of the old tennis ball with the warm clay or play dough.
3. Use the pencil to poke holes all over the surface.
4. Leave the ball to dry—this will take up to one day.

163 WEIGHT UP!

You would have to be six times heavier on the moon to weigh as much as you do on Earth!

WHAT'S THE SCIENCE?

The strength of gravity on the moon is about one sixth of that on Earth. The force of gravity pulling us down is what determines our weight. Therefore, if you went to the moon you would weigh one sixth of what you weigh on Earth.

Materials

- bathroom scale
- calculator

Steps

1. Weigh yourself on your bathroom scale.
2. Divide your weight by six.
3. That is how much you would weigh on the moon.

164 HOLY IMPACT!

Time to make some moon dust!

WHAT'S THE SCIENCE?

The moon is covered in bowl-like holes called craters. Craters are a bit like scars on the moon's surface. They are caused when objects in space, such as meteors, crash into the moon.

Materials

- newspaper
- baking pan
- flour
- cocoa powder
- pepper
- cinnamon
- powdered/icing sugar
- marble
- small objects such as coins, grapes, or rocks

Steps

1. Lay newspaper down on the floor and set the baking pan on top of it.
2. Cover the base of the pan with an even 2-in (5-cm) of flour.
3. Dust a layer of cocoa powder on top of the flour. Repeat with pepper, then cinnamon, then powdered/icing sugar.
4. Hold the marble waist-high, then drop it onto the tray. Check out the crater you made!
5. Drop a few other objects to make more craters!

165 STAR SHOW

Just like people, stars hang out in groups!

WHAT'S THE SCIENCE?

A group of stars that is visible within a particular part of the night sky is called a **constellation**. Constellations are often named after animals, mythological creatures, and scientific instruments. They are visible between sunset and sunrise. As Earth rotates, different constellations can be seen.

Materials

- shoebox
- image of your favorite constellation
- marker
- sharp pencil
- flashlight/torch
- scissors

Steps

1. Copy the pattern of your constellation onto the side of the shoebox.
2. With a sharp pencil, poke a small hole in the shoebox where each star in your constellation appears.
3. On the opposite side of the shoebox, trace around the head of the flashlight/torch, then cut a hole and fit the flashlight into the box.
4. In a dark room, point the flashlight toward the roof or a wall and turn it on. What do you see?

166 STELLAR SNACK

Constellations are amazing—and delicious, too!

WHAT'S THE SCIENCE?

Some constellations seen in the Northern Hemisphere are also visible in the Southern Hemisphere at certain times of the year. Examples are:
- Orion, the hunter
- Pegasus, the flying horse
- Ursa Major, the big bear
- Ursa Minor, the little bear

Other constellations are visible mainly in the Southern Hemisphere and in the Northern Hemisphere at certain times of year. Examples are:
- Apus, the bird of paradise
- Crux, the southern cross
- Hydrus, the water snake
- Pictor, the easel

DID YOU KNOW?

Sirius is the brightest star we can see. Its name comes from the Greek word Seirios— which means "glowing" or "scorcher."

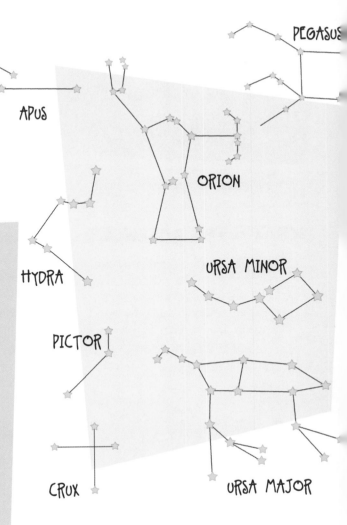

Materials

- bag of mini marshmallows
- several dozen toothpicks

Steps

1. Choose one of the constellations from the list above that you would like to recreate with your marshmallows.

2. Build the constellation, using marshmallows for the stars and joining them with toothpicks to represent the areas between the stars.

167 NIGHT LIGHTS

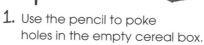

Twinkle, twinkle, little star …

WHAT'S THE SCIENCE?

Light refracts when it passes through materials with varying densities. When starlight passes through Earth's atmosphere it refracts because the atmosphere is made up of different materials. This is why some stars appear to twinkle.

Materials

- sharp pencil
- empty cereal box
- flashlight/torch
- stovetop

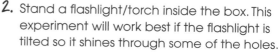

Steps

1. Use the pencil to poke holes in the empty cereal box.

2. Stand a flashlight/torch inside the box. This experiment will work best if the flashlight is tilted so it shines through some of the holes.

3. Close the top of the box, then stand it next to the stovetop. (Make sure it is not touching the burners.) Ask an adult to help you turn the burner on. Stand so the burner is between you and the box, and watch the box.

4. As the heat rises from the burner, your stars will begin to shimmer and twinkle.

168 COSMO COUNT

Ever wondered how many stars are visible in the entire night sky?

WHAT'S THE SCIENCE?

There are approximately 100 billion stars in the Milky Way **galaxy**. From Earth, we can only see a fraction of that number due to local weather conditions and our limited view. This activity will help you get a rough estimate of what you can see from your neighborhood.

Materials

- adult helper
- toilet paper tube
- paper and pen
- calculator

Steps

1. Ask an adult to go outside with you on a dark, clear night.

2. Looking through the paper tube with one eye, count all the stars you see while your helper records the number. To make this easier, divide the sky that is visible to you into 10 sections and count the stars in each section.

3. Now, using a calculator, add up the stars counted in each section to get the total number. Think about how many stars you can see from your area alone, and then think about how many must be visible over the entire world!

169 TWINKLE TIME

Let the stars reveal themselves to you—which ones are brightest?

WHAT'S THE SCIENCE?

A star's brightness is referred to as its magnitude. "Apparent magnitude" is how bright it appears when viewed from Earth. "Absolute magnitude" is its real brightness. Some stars appear bright to us because they are very nearby. Other distant stars appear bright because they are so hot and large.

Materials

- stanley knife (ask an adult for help)
- piece of cardboard
- tape
- colored cellophane sheets

Steps

1. Use the knife to cut four rectangular holes, roughly 2 x 4 in (5 x 10 cm), side by side in the cardboard.
2. Tape one piece of cellophane over all four holes.
3. Now tape a second piece over just three of the holes.
4. Next, tape a third piece over two of those three holes.
5. Lastly, tape a fourth piece over one of those last two holes.
6. Take your viewer outside and hold it up to the sky. Note what happens when you look through a hole with more cellophane sheets. (You will only be able to see light from the very brightest stars.)

170 THE HOLE PICTURE

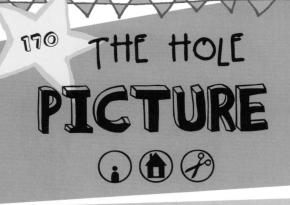

Black holes are like the vacuum cleaners of outer space!

WHAT'S THE SCIENCE?

Black holes are a bit like vacuum cleaners— they clean up **debris** in outer space. However, instead of using suction, black holes rely on gravity to pull things toward them. Because black holes suck in light, astronomers can't see them. They have to look for gravity swirling around the hole, just as water does around a bath plughole.

Materials

- magnifying glass
- newspaper

Steps

1. Hold your magnifying glass just above the newspaper.
2. Move it back and forth slowly.
3. What you see is what astronomers see when they look at black holes.

171 GALAXY GIRL

Go the distance with this astronomically cool experiment!

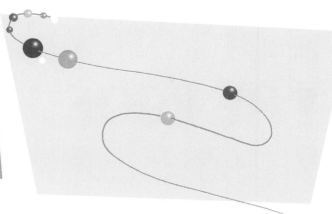

WHAT'S THE SCIENCE?

Space is huge—so huge that miles and kilometers are too small to measure distances. Instead, scientists use something called an AU, an "astronomical unit." The average distance between Earth and the sun is one AU, which is equal to 93 million mi, or 149 million km.

DID YOU KNOW?

If you were traveling 100 mph (160 kph), you would have to travel for more than 100 years to cover the distance of 1 AU!

Materials

- a large space to spread out your solar system, such as a large room, a yard, or a field
- 9 beads (use various colors and sizes to make each planet unique)
- a long piece of string, at least 16 ½ ft (5 m) long
- a metric ruler
- tape that you can write on

Steps

1. Using the chart below, look at the number of AU each planet is from the sun. In this chart, 1 AU is equal to 10 cm.

   If the Earth is at 1 AU, then the other planets are:

   Mercury 0.4 AU = 4 cm

   Venus 0.7 AU = 7 cm

   Earth 1 AU = 10 cm

   Mars 1.5 AU = 15 cm

   Jupiter 5.5 AU = 55 cm

   Saturn 10 AU = 100 cm, or 1 m

   Uranus 20.1 AU = 201 cm, or about 2 m

   Neptune 30.4 AU = 304 cm or about 3 m

   Pluto 49.3 AU = 493 cm or about 5 m

2. Place beads on your string to represent the planets. Secure them with tape so they don't slide along the string, then label each one. This model will give you an idea of the distances between the planets. (It's amazing to think that the four inner planets are so close!)

172 RAISIN THE ROOF

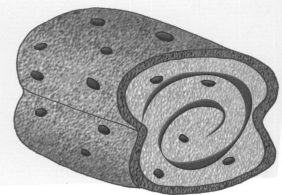

Sometimes a little midnight snack can go a very long way!

WHAT'S THE SCIENCE?

About 13 billion years ago, **cosmologists** believe there was a "big bang." This was the explosive beginning of the universe as we know it. As the universe expanded—and matter, stars, galaxies, and **nebulae** were born—each part of the universe spread outward away from the explosion. In this experiment, the raisins move away from each other as the dough expands, just as the parts of the universe spread apart.

DID YOU KNOW?

Named after Edwin Hubble (1889–1953), the Hubble Telescope sits outside Earth's atmosphere, taking beautiful pictures of deep space objects. Hubble uses observations of galaxies and light to show that our universe is constantly expanding.

Materials

- small bowl
- 1 teaspoon baking soda/bicarbonate of soda
- 1 cup boiling water
- medium bowl
- 1 ½ cups all purpose/plain flour, plus a little extra
- ½ teaspoon salt
- ½ cup sugar
- 1 beaten egg
- 1 tablespoon vegetable oil
- baking pan
- 1 dab of butter (approx. the same amount you would use to butter a slice of toast)
- 1 cup raisins
- 1 toothpick
- wire rack

Steps

1. Preheat your oven to 350° F (180° C).
2. In the small bowl, mix together the baking soda/bicarbonate of soda and boiling water. Leave for 30 minutes.
3. In a medium bowl, mix together the flour, salt, and sugar. Add baking soda mixture.
4. Stir in the egg and oil, mixing well.
5. Grease the baking pan with butter, then sprinkle with flour.
6. Pour in the dough.
7. Fold the raisins into the center of the dough.
8. Bake the dough for 45 minutes or until golden brown. To test if cooked, insert a toothpick into the center. If it comes out clean, the bread is done.
9. Allow the bread to cool for 10 minutes in the pan, and then transfer to a wire rack to cool completely.
10. Cut the dough and observe how the raisins moved apart as the dough expanded.

173 A STAR IS BORN

Make big stuff happen in one little dish!

WHAT'S THE SCIENCE?

Galaxies live together in clusters just like cows live in herds. Sometimes they bump into each other and disturb each other's shape. When this happens it can cause new stars to be born—creating an amazing display of fireworks! Sometimes within a galaxy, dust, gas, and stars form into spiral arms that reach outward. When this happens, a galaxy becomes a "**spiral galaxy**."

Materials

- shallow dish
- coin
- water
- small circles of paper (confetti)

Steps

1. Sit the dish on the coin so you can spin it easily.
2. Pour about 0.5 in (1 cm) of water into the dish.
3. Gently sprinkle the confetti in the middle of the dish.
4. Slowly spin the dish and watch what happens to the paper in the middle.

174 STAR GAZERS

Don't let light pollution stop you from enjoying a star-filled sky!

WHAT'S THE SCIENCE?

Light pollution makes it difficult to see the stars at night. There are two types of light pollution: sky glow and local glare. Sky glow is the orange glow caused by hundreds or thousands of lights in places like buildings, roads, and parking lots. Local glare comes from local sources, such as a streetlight or a neighbor's window.

Materials

- glue
- large piece of black paper or cardboard
- glitter
- scissors
- shiny metallic paper
- silver metallic paint
- flashlight/torch

Steps

1. Use the glue to create night sky patterns on the piece of paper.
2. Sprinkle glitter over the glue.
3. Cut stars from the metallic paper and stick them on the paper.
4. Use the silver metallic paint to outline your stars.
5. Stick the paper on your bedroom ceiling. (Ask an adult first.)
6. Before you go to bed, shine your torch on your ceiling to see your sky.
7. Now turn the light on. Do the stars still twinkle as much?

175 UNDER THE NIGHT SKY

Forget singing in the rain—
try singing under the stars instead!

Materials

- book or star chart of constellations (optional)
- paper and pencil
- black umbrella
- chalk

WHAT'S THE SCIENCE?

When we study the sky over a period of time, the constellations above us seem to be moving. This is an example of "apparent motion." The stars are not actually moving—we are! Earth rotates on its axis. As Earth rotates from west to east, the constellations appear to travel in the other direction—from east to west.

Steps

1. Sketch the night sky or copy some of the constellations from a book or star chart onto a piece of paper.
2. Using chalk, copy the images onto the inside of the black umbrella.
3. Stand under the umbrella and slowly turn it.

176 DUST CLOUDS

Life goes on—even for stars!

Materials

- toothbrush
- silver and white paint
- black cardboard
- red, purple, blue, and green pastels
- glue
- sequins

WHAT'S THE SCIENCE?

When stars die, they get rid of their outer layers. These form clouds of dust and gas. These clouds glow and are called "planetary nebulae." They are often in the shape of a bubble or ring.

Steps

1. Use the toothbrush to flick spots of silver and white paint onto the black cardboard.
2. Draw a circle on the paper with the pastels and then smudge the colors so they mix together.
3. Glue some sequins onto your nebula.

⭐ 177 AGE GAUGE

(i) (🏠) (✂️)

Check out what your age would be on different planets!

$$10 \div 1.88 = ?$$

WHAT'S THE SCIENCE?

We measure our age in years, months, and days. Each year we live represents one trip around the sun on our "spaceship," Earth! However, if you lived on Mars, a year would last almost twice as long—686.9 days! If you are ten Earth years old now, that would make you just five Mars years old! Check out this chart to learn how old you would be on other planets.

PLANET	TIME IT TAKES TO COMPLETE ONE REVOLUTION
Mercury	0.241 Earth years (87.9 Earth days)
Venus	0.615 Earth years (224.7 Earth days)
Earth	1 Earth year (365.25 Earth days)
Mars	1.88 Earth years (686.9 Earth days)
Jupiter	11.9 Earth years (4343.5 Earth days)
Saturn	29.5 Earth years (10 767.5 Earth days)
Uranus	84.0 Earth years (30 660 Earth days)
Neptune	164.8 Earth years (60 152 Earth days)
Pluto	248.5 Earth years (90 702.5 Earth days)

Materials

- paper
- pen
- calculator

Steps

1. Enter your age into the calculator.
2. Divide that number by the time it takes for the planet to complete one revolution. (For example, if you are ten and you want to work out how old you would be on Mars you would press 10/1.88 = 5.32 years old!)
3. Now you know how old you would be if you lived on another planet!

DID YOU KNOW?

There are eight planets in our solar system (Pluto is a dwarf planet). Saturn is the second biggest planet. But did you know it is also the lightest planet? In fact, it is the only planet in our solar system that could float in water.

178 UNDER PRESSURE

Feeling the pressure?

WHAT'S THE SCIENCE?

Each planet has its own atmospheric pressure. We don't notice it on Earth because we are used to it. Atmosphere pressure is measured in units called atms. The typical pressure on Mars is only one tenth of the pressure on Earth. This is because the atmosphere on Mars is made of different materials, and is "higher" than Earth's atmosphere—11 km above the planet, compared to Earth's 7 km.

Materials

- bathtub
- shallow pan
- deep pan
- water

Steps

1. Fill the bathtub, the shallow pan, and the deep pan with water.

2. Place your hand, palm side down, into the water in each pan. Now do the same in the bathtub. What differences do you feel? Water puts pressure on your hand just like the atmosphere does. With more water, you feel more pressure!

179 SPUD BUDS

These potatoes are truly out-of-this-world!

WHAT'S THE SCIENCE?

Asteroids are chunks of rock that orbit in space. Most of them orbit the sun in an area called the asteroid belt, which sits between Mars and Jupiter. But some asteroids have orbits that cross or come close to Earth's orbit. Some asteroids are also called "planetoids" because they are large enough to be round.

Materials

- butter
- baking tray
- 4–8 cups of mashed potatoes
- milk
- oven mitt

Steps

1. Preheat your oven to 375° F (190° C).

2. Grease the baking tray with the butter.

3. Take a handful of mashed potato and mold it into an interesting shape. Poke dents in it for craters. (If the mashed potato is too dry, add a little milk.)

4. Set the asteroid on the baking tray. Make some more.

5. Bake your asteroids for 20–25 minutes, or until they are brown.

6. Using an oven mitt, remove the tray from the oven (ask an adult for help). Transfer the asteroids to a serving plate. Enjoy!

180 RING AROUND THE PLANET

Swirling clouds can be seen as bands on Jupiter!

WHAT'S THE SCIENCE?

Pictures of Jupiter show that its surface is made up of bands of clouds. These clouds are made of different chemicals, including ammonia and water crystals.

Materials

- shallow tray
- water
- liquid oil paints
- pointer, such as a skewer or drinking straw
- paper

Steps

1. Fill the shallow tray with some water.
2. Pour some of the liquid oil paint onto the water.
3. Drag the pointer across the floating paints in parallel lines to form bands.
4. Lay the sheet of paper on top of the water so that it picks up the paints.
5. Now you have an image of Jupiter's clouds!

181 MARTIAN MAKER

Make a being that might stand a chance of living and surviving on Mars!

WHAT'S THE SCIENCE?

NASA says that Mars is an "unfriendly planet" for life. It has no liquid water to support living things. It does not have a protective **ozone layer**. It is home to massive seasonal sand storms. And it has massive volcanoes—including the largest one in our solar system, Olympus Mons!

Materials

- clay
- paint
- marker pens
- things to decorate with (string, buttons, etc.)

Steps

1. Think about the living conditions on Mars. What type of creature might actually be able to live there? What would it need in order to survive?
2. Design a Martian that you think could survive in the harsh environment on Mars.
3. Make a Martian out of clay. Let the clay harden.
4. Decorate your Martian using the paint, pens, and decorations.

182 DUST 'N' RUST

Most people try to get rid of rust—but you're going to make some!

WHAT'S THE SCIENCE?

Imagine living on Mars and studying it up close. Astronauts living on the red surface would have one big problem to deal with—rust! Mars is covered in a layer of **iron oxide**, which produces rust. This layer of rust is what gives Mars its red color. This iron collected on the surface of the planet when it first formed, and reacted with carbon dioxide in the atmosphere to make rust.

Materials

- 4 clear cups (glass or plastic)
- ½ cup water
- ¼ cup vinegar
- ½ cup sand
- 4 iron nails or strips of iron

Steps

1. Place the water, vinegar, and sand in one cup each. Leave the fourth cup empty.
2. Stand a nail or strip of iron in each cup so that it is half submerged and half above the surface.
3. Leave the nails in the cups for one week. Check them regularly to see how they change. What do you see?

She did it!

Barbara Cohen

Growing up, Dr. Barbara Cohen spent her time writing, reading, and playing music. She had no idea she would become a scientist! But one day she saw a TV show about the spacecraft *Voyager* visiting planets, and she couldn't believe how beautiful the planets looked. She signed up for a geology class in college and discovered a passion for studying rocks. Barbara began experimenting with techniques and instruments that helped her to learn all about how and where a rock formed. Barbara is now a planetary scientist at NASA's Marshall Space Flight Center. She is part of the team working on the Mars Exploration Rovers *Spirit* and *Opportunity*. She even has an asteroid named after herself (Asteroid 6816 Barbcohen)!

183 SHINE A LIGHT!

What's the message? Tune in to a satellite to find out!

WHAT'S THE SCIENCE?

Satellites send information to one another—sometimes from the other side of the planet! They work almost like mirrors in space, bouncing pictures and data between one another at the speed of light. Satellites are used in military planning, navigational assistance, and weather forecasting. They are wide, shallow dishes, designed to catch as many signals as possible.

Materials

- three friends
- flashlight/torch
- mirror

Steps

1. Position three people so that they make a large triangle.
2. Give each person a job: the caller, the receiver, and the satellite.
3. Give the "caller" the flashlight/torch, and give the "satellite" the mirror.
4. Turn the light off and ask the caller to shine their flashlight onto the mirror. Have the person holding the mirror shine the light onto the receiver.

184 MEET A METEOR!

The sky is falling! The sky is falling!

WHAT'S THE SCIENCE?

Meteors are small rock-like chunks that break off from comets and other **celestial** debris. As they enter Earth's atmosphere, they appear to glow. The **friction** of the rock rubs against the atmosphere, causing heat and light. In this experiment, the seltzer bubbles "trail" in the water, following the tablet, just as a meteor shooting through the sky leaves a glow in its wake.

Materials

- plastic bottle
- water
- ½ seltzer tablet

Steps

1. Fill up the plastic bottle with water.
2. Drop the tablet into the water and watch what happens.

DID YOU KNOW?

Meteors that fall on Earth rarely do any damage, as they are usually so small. But about 65 million years ago an enormous meteor—about 8 mi (13 km) across—crashed into Earth and caused a crater that sent thousands of tons of dust into the air.

185 BLAST OFF!

3, 2, 1 … BLAST OFF!

WHAT'S THE SCIENCE?

Rockets transport astronauts into space. A rocket is launched by an action and a reaction. The gas escaping the balloon represents the action. The balloon moving in the opposite direction represents the reaction. During blast-off, the faster the gas leaves a rocket, the faster it will push off!

Materials

- scissors
- 1 large disposable paper or plastic drinking cup
- sticky tape
- 1 round balloon

Steps

1. Carefully cut the bottom out of the cup.
2. Tape the round balloon inside the cup and blow up the balloon.
3. Hold the end of the round balloon closed but do not tie.
4. Hold the rocket so it is facing the sky.
5. Let go of the balloon.

186 YOU-NIVERSE

Send a message about yourself—far into the future!

WHAT'S THE SCIENCE?

When the *Voyager* spacecraft was launched in 1977, it carried with it a phonograph/vinyl record with sounds and images depicting life on Earth. They were intended for **extraterrestrial** life forms who might find them. The records were one of the first attempts to communicate with others about our planet.

Materials

- paper
- markers and crayons
- favorite items
- recorder and tape or CD
- box

Steps

1. Draw some pictures of your life on Earth, such as yourself, your family, and your home, as well as some "bigger" things, such as your country and your continent.
2. Collect current objects, such as toys, a magazine or newspaper, CDs, photos.
3. Record a message for someone who might hear it a long way into the future.
4. Put all of the items in a box and save it. Perhaps your box will serve as an important source of information to someone—or some*thing*—in the future!

187 SUPER SUITS

Getting dressed takes on a whole new meaning when you're an astronaut!

WHAT'S THE SCIENCE?

Spacesuits make it very hard for astronauts to work in space. The heavy suits tire astronauts quickly and make movement difficult. But spacesuits protect astronauts from the airless vacuum of space. They create Earth-like conditions inside, providing the right temperature, pressure, and protection against solar radiation. Without the suits, the astronauts would die.

Materials

- nuts and bolts
- rubber gloves
- big bowl
- water

DID YOU KNOW?

Spacesuits are like individual spacecraft, providing astronauts with warmth, oxygen, and power.

Steps

1. Place the nuts and bolts onto a table and try picking them up and screwing them together.

2. Now put on the rubber gloves (your own version of spacesuit gloves) and try to do the same thing.

3. Fill the bowl with water. Add the nuts and bolts.

4. Still wearing the gloves, try to pick up the nuts and bolts and screw them together under the water.

188 FOOD FREEZE

Would you like to eat like an astronaut?

WHAT'S THE SCIENCE?

When they are on missions, astronauts eat **space food**. Space food must be nutritious and easy to digest. It must also be light, well-packaged, and easy to serve and store. Space foods are **rehydratable** and **thermostabilized**. Rehydratable foods do not weigh very much, and thermostabilized foods don't contain bacteria, so they will not spoil.

Materials
- baby food or pureed vegetables
- microwave oven
- microwave-safe plastic bag

Steps

1. Place the baby food or pureed vegetables into a microwave-safe plastic bag.
2. Freeze the food.
3. Once frozen, put the plastic bag into the microwave and heat the food. Careful—the food will be hot!
4. Eat your space food!

DID YOU KNOW?

Space crews eat three meals a day. They can choose from about 70 different menus. The meals are planned before the mission begins.

189

SPOT ON

Check out one of the greatest human accomplishments of all time!

WHAT'S THE SCIENCE?

The International Space Station is a research laboratory that orbits Earth. Astronauts from all around the world live and work on the station, studying how humans and other materials respond to life in **micro-gravity**. The ISS is made of many different sections, all linked together like a giant Lego robot. Solar panels power the station—the **solar array** has a wingspan longer than a Boeing 777 200/300's!

Materials

- Internet access
- a clear, dark night
- binoculars (optional)

Steps

1. Use the NASA Website to find out when the ISS will be flying near your area. Go to http://spaceflight1.nasa.gov/realdata/sightings/

2. When the ISS will be passing over you, go outside and get ready to watch for it. Try to find a place with very little light pollution. Turn out any nearby lights if you can. Now study the sky.

3. When you look at the stars, you can see small points of light move across the sky. These are not stars—it takes hours to see stars move across the sky—they are satellites, orbiting Earth. One of those satellites will be the ISS!

190

ROVER— READY

Audition your toys for the role of Mars rover!

WHAT'S THE SCIENCE?

Rovers do what their name suggests—they rove! *Spirit, Opportunity, Sojourner,* and *Pathfinder* have all sent back incredible data and pictures of Mars. The rovers are controlled by scientists on Earth. They use scientific instruments to learn about the surface of the planet they are exploring. Rovers are designed to handle very fine sand when roving on Mars.

Materials

- 2 cups sand
- 2 cups rice
- 2 cups coarse dirt or gravel
- 3 cookie trays
- 3–4 toys with four wheels, such as cars, trucks, or even ducks!
- a long piece of string
- pen and paper
- water

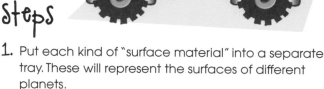

Steps

1. Put each kind of "surface material" into a separate tray. These will represent the surfaces of different planets.

2. Tie your first toy to the string and slowly drag it across each surface. Record how each toy travelled across the surfaces. Did the sand get stuck in the wheels? Did the car drag too much gravel when it moved? Repeat with each of the toys.

3. Add water to each surface then test the vehicles again. How did they respond?

191 ALPHA-SPACE

Materials

- notebook
- colored pencils
- this book

Steps

Make a *Super Space Dictionary* to teach your friends and family all about the wonderful things you learned in this chapter.

Refer to the "Wonder Words" glossary on the next pages if you need to remember definitions. Don't forget to illustrate your dictionary!

Be sure to include these 20 terms in your illustrated space dictionary!

1. asteroid
2. astronaut
3. atmosphere
4. black hole
5. comet
6. constellation
7. crater
8. dwarf planet
9. galaxy
10. meteor
11. moon
12. moon rocks
13. orbit
14. planets
15. rocket
16. space food
17. spiral galaxy
18. star
19. sun
20. telescope

DID YOU KNOW?

A rover that launched in 2011 was named Curiosity by a 6th grader, Clara Ma, from Kansas, who won a naming contest held by NASA. She even got to sign it!

WONDER WORDS

absorb—To take in.

apex—The highest point.

asteroids—Rocks that usually orbit the space between Mars and Jupiter, with diameters ranging from less than 0.6 mi to nearly 500 mi (1 km–800 km) .

astronauts—Scientists who travel on spacecraft.

astronomers—Scientists who study the universe.

atmosphere—The mixture of gases that surrounds celestial bodies, such as planets.

axis—A straight line around which something rotates.

black holes—Invisible regions in space with gravitational fields so strong that light cannot escape from them.

celestial—Relating to the stars.

comets—Masses of rocky material and ice that orbit the solar system. When close to the sun, their cloudy tails are visible through a telescope.

constellation—One of 88 star formations.

cosmologists—Scientists who study the structures and characteristics of the universe.

craters—Bowl-shaped depressions caused by the impacts of rocks and meteorites.

debris—The scattered remains of something broken or destroyed.

dense—Tightly packed with molecules.

dwarf planet—A celestial body that orbits the sun, but does not orbit alone.

elements—The substances that make up matter. Each element has a unique atomic structure.

equator—An imaginary line that circles Earth at its center.

extraterrestrial—Originating or existing beyond Earth or its atmosphere.

frequencies—Measures of how often a wave "vibrates" in a given amount of time. For example, light waves travel in Hz, or waves per second.

friction—Resistance caused by one object rubbing against another.

fulcrum—The point on which a lever pivots.

galaxy—Groups of stars in our universe that revolve around a central point. Some galaxies, like our Milky Way, can have as many as 300 billion stars.

gravity—A force of attraction between atoms. The greater an object's mass, the stronger its gravitational pull.

iron oxide—Otherwise known as rust, the reddish material that forms when iron is exposed to oxygen.

lenses—Curved pieces of glass or plastic that bend light rays in order to form images.

magnitude—The brightness of a star.

matter—The substance that makes up a physical object.

meteors—Small bodies of matter that enter Earth's atmosphere and glow brightly, briefly, due to heat caused by friction.

micro-gravity—Having little to no gravitational force.

moon rocks—Rocks found on the moon.

moons—Natural satellites that revolve around a planet.

nebulae—Large clouds of gas and/or dust in space where stars are born.

orbit—The path a planet follows around a star or another planet. Usually an ellipse, or oval.

ozone layer—A layer of atmosphere 20–30 mi (30–50 km) above Earth that prevents most of the sun's ultraviolet radiation from entering Earth's lower atmosphere.

parallax—The apparent alteration of the position of an object caused by the change in position of someone looking at the object.

photometry—A field of astronomy focused on electromagnetic radiation and its intensity.

planets—Planets are bodies that orbit the sun, have enough gravity for their mass to form a round ball, and do not have any other objects in their orbits.

plasma—Charged particles under extreme heat, such as those in the sun, that resemble gas and conduct electricity.

poles—The northernmost and southernmost points on Earth, found at either end of Earth's axis.

reflect—To bounce back light, heat, or sound waves from a surface.

refracting—Bending light as it passes from one medium to another.

regolith—The layer of loose material that covers solid rock.

rehydratable—A food type that has been freeze-dried and can be eaten after adding hot water.

revolves—Travels in an orbit.

rockets—Human-run, robotic or remote-controlled machines that record and capture information from objects outside of Earth's atmosphere. They can contain instruments that are used to orbit, land, or impact another solar system object, or can transport humans to the International Space Station. They are propelled into space using fuel that can break through Earth's gravitational pull.

rotation—The process of turning, usually on an axis.

Solar array—A system or collection of solar panels that convert sunlight into electricity.

Solar radiation—Radiant energy that is emitted by the sun in one of several forms, such as electromagnetic energy, visible light, or ultraviolet light.

Space food—Food products specifically designed for astronauts to consume in outer space.

Spiral galaxy—A galaxy that resembles a disk with a bulge in its center, made up mostly of old stars, with two brightly lit spiral arms made up mostly of younger stars.

star—A ball of gases, mostly hydrogen and helium, that emits heat and light due to nuclear fusion.

Sun—A star around which planets revolve and from which they receive heat and light.

telescopes—Instruments with mirrors or lenses that focus light rays, making it possible to view distant objects.

thermostabilized—Treated with heat so the food can be stored safely at moderate temperatures without going bad.

wavelengths—The distance between corresponding points in a wave pattern.

WILD CHILD
LIFE SCIENCES

192

CLASS ACT

Get to know your animal groups!

WHAT'S THE SCIENCE?

Scientists use **classification** to identify different kinds of animals. Animals can be classified into six groups. **Birds** are **warm-blooded** and have feathers and lay eggs. **Mammals** are warm-blooded and most give birth to live young. **Reptiles** are **cold-blooded** and lay eggs. **Amphibians** are cold-blooded and live in water and on land. **Fish** are cold-blooded and breathe underwater using their **gills**. **Invertebrates** are animals that do not have backbones, such as insects and worms.

Materials

- old magazines
- scissors
- a friend

Steps

1. Cut out all the animal pictures you can find in the magazines.
2. Decide how you are going to classify the animals. You could sort them by the number of legs they have; where they live; whether they are **carnivores** or **herbivores**; fast or slow; land or sea animals, and so on.
3. Ask your friend to guess how you classified the animals. See if you can trick them by using categories such as **marsupials** or **monotremes**.
4. Don't forget to let your friend have a turn at classifying the animals, too. You could also play this game with plants or insects.

193

CRITTER COLLECTION

It's time to get down and dirty with some invertebrates!

Materials

- bucket
- soil
- sieve
- piece of white paper
- magnifying glass

Steps

1. Take your bucket outside and fill it with soil. If possible, collect the soil from around a tree and under dead leaves.
2. Pour some soil into the sieve. Shake it over the piece of paper.
3. Use the magnifying glass to look at the soil on the paper. Do you see small animals running across the paper?

WHAT'S THE SCIENCE?

Soil is home to millions of living things—many of which are **microscopic**, such as **bacteria** and **fungi**. Soil is also home to different kinds of invertebrates. Invertebrates are animals that don't have backbones, such as insects, spiders and worms. Invertebrates feed on the bacteria and fungi that live in soil.

194 AWESOME ARACHNIDS

What's the difference between spiders and insects? It's all in the legs!

WHAT'S THE SCIENCE?

Both insects and spiders belong to the **phyla "arthropod."** However, even though they are both arthropods, they are not the same. Insects have six legs and three parts to their body. Spiders have eight legs and two parts to their body. Spiders are a kind of creature called an "**arachnid.**"

Materials

- dead spider (ask an adult to make sure) or toy spider. Do not pick up a live spider—it may be poisonous.
- dead fly (don't touch the fly, just study it), or toy fly

Steps

1. Count the number of legs on the spider. There should be eight.
2. Now count the number of legs on the fly.
3. Can you see the different sections of each creature's body? How many sections does each of them have?

195 EYE SEE YOU!

Spiders could be spying on you in the darkness!

WHAT'S THE SCIENCE?

Spiders' eyes "shine" at night. Behind the **retina** of a spider's eye is a shiny layer, called a tapetum. A tapetum allows a spider's eye to collect more light, which helps it to hunt in the dark.

DID YOU KNOW?

*Alligators, cats, dogs, deer, and raccoons all have tapetums, too! Tapetums are helpful to **nocturnal** animals.*

Materials

- an adult
- flashlight/torch

Steps

1. Take an adult and a flashlight/torch outside with you at night. Hold the flashlight next to your head, at the same height as your eye, and point it forward.
2. Slowly turn around, examining your surroundings. Look closely at areas where you see flowers and grass.
3. If you see bright pinpoints of light, stop turning and move in closer. What are they? Water drops? Or spiders' eyes?!

196 WONDER WEB

Make a web like a garden spider would!

WHAT'S THE SCIENCE?

Spiders spin webs to catch their **prey**. The biggest, roundest spiderwebs are made by garden spiders. Garden spiders make their webs by releasing silk from **spinnerets** while jumping between branches. A garden spider's web has a supportive, circular "thread path" in its center. The web can be up to 4 ft (1.2 m) across!

DID YOU KNOW?

When a garden spider does not want prey that is trapped in its web, it will cut off that section of the web and let it fall.

Materials

- 6 chairs
- ball of string

Steps

1. Arrange the chairs in a circle with one in the center.

2. Knot the string around the leg of one chair, then carry the string to a second chair and loop it around an arm or through the back.

3. Repeat this in a pattern, looping the string to different chairs and returning to the center every so often before moving back out. Continue until the string has looped through each chair at least three times.

4. Cut the string and tie the loose end.

5. Act like a spider and crawl around, over, through, and under your new web!

She did it!

DIAN FOSSEY

From the time that she was a young girl, Dian had a passion for animals. In college, she studied business at her stepfather's request, but never lost her love of animals, and soon entered a pre-veterinary program. Dian planned her first trip to Africa after seeing photos from a friend's vacation. Dian began working on gorilla conservation, and became an expert **primatologist** and **zoologist**. Dian remained in Africa studying gorillas for 18 years. She is known worldwide for her incredible efforts to save mountain gorillas from extinction.

197 BUZZY BEES

How do you make a bee happy?
Color and sweetness, of course!

WHAT'S THE SCIENCE?

Bees are attracted to the sweetness of the sugar. They are also drawn to bright colors. Flowers rely on bees for **pollination**. They lure bees with their bright colors and sweet fragrances. As a bee forages for nectar within a flower's center, it will brush against the flower's anthers (the pollen-bearing parts of a flower) and release thousands of male pollen particles—and play a key part in the survival of the flower species.

Materials

- 5 pieces of different-colored strong cardboard (including 1 black and 1 white piece)
- scissors
- 5 drinking straws
- tape
- sugar
- water
- 3 plastic lids from small jars or soft drink bottles
- salt
- sweet soft drink
- notebook
- pencil

Steps

1. Cut each piece of cardboard into a flower shape. The flowers should have large petals.

2. Using the scissors, cut four small slits in one end of each drinking straw. Squash the cut end of each straw against the back of a flower so it makes a star shape. Tape the straw to the cardboard.

3. Mix a tiny amount of sugar and water until you have a sticky paste. Place the paste in one of the lids. Repeat with the salt, and place it in another lid.

4. Pour a small amount of soft drink into another lid.

5. Stick each lid to the center of a flower using a rolled up ball of tape. Two flowers will not have a lid.

6. 'Plant' your flowers outside. Observe and record which flower the bees are most attracted to. What color is it? What is in the cap on that flower?

7. Place the lids on different flowers. Which flower are the bees most attracted to now?

DID YOU KNOW?

Honeybees "dance" to tell each other where flowers are located!

198 THAT BITES!

Getting mosquito bites just really ... well ... bites!

WHAT'S THE SCIENCE?

Mosquitoes are also known as "blood suckers!" When a mosquito lands on you, it uses its long nose (called a **proboscis**) to break the skin and suck up blood. The small hole it makes becomes itchy. Insects' blood is called hemolymph. It can be many colors, depending on the insect: clear, green, yellow, or bluish. The red blood you see when you squash a mosquito is mammal blood; possibly your own!

Materials

- magnifying glass
- piece of paper
- insect bite cream

NOTE: Do not try this experiment if you are allergic to mosquitoes or if you live in an area that is prone to mosquito-borne illnesses.

Steps

1. On a warm night, wear a T-shirt so that the skin on your arms is exposed.
2. Sit outside near a light or lamp. Make sure the magnifying glass and piece of paper are nearby.
3. Wait until a mosquito lands on your arm. Using your free hand, quickly pick up the magnifying glass and use it to watch the mosquito.
4. Watch closely how it bites you.
5. Now squash it with the piece of paper. What happens?
6. Don't forget to put some cream on the bite to stop it itching!

199 SUPER SMELLERS

Could you survive using only your sense of smell?

WHAT'S THE SCIENCE?

Many species, such as ants, rely on smell and sensing vibrations to find food. Ants live underground, where they can't rely on their sight because it is so dark. Other animals that rely heavily on smell include moles and dogs.

Materials

- partner
- blindfold
- range of different foods

Steps

1. Have your partner blindfold you.
2. Ask them to place the food in different places around the room.
3. Walk around the room using your hands and your nose to see if you can find any of the food. When you find some, pick it up and see if you can identify it.

200

ENCH—ANT—ING!

Share your snacks—
and make some friends!

Materials

- small pieces of apple
- piece of bread, torn into chunks
- small pieces of potato
- small amount of sugar

WHAT'S THE SCIENCE?

Ants mostly eat sugary and greasy foods, seeking out whatever is in season. The sweetness of the apple gives off a strong scent that attracts the ants. If a queen is laying eggs, worker ants will bring her foods that are higher in **protein**.

Steps

1. Place each different type of food in a different place around the garden or park.
2. Watch to see which kind of food attracts more ants.

201

PILL BUG

PALACE

Meet a "bug" that's not
actually a bug at all!

WHAT'S THE SCIENCE?

Pill bugs (also known as slaters) are not actually insects—they're **crustaceans**. Look closely and you will see that they closely resemble other crustaceans, such as crayfish and shrimp. Pill bugs breathe through gills and require moist environments in order to breathe. But unlike many of their marine relatives, pill bugs cannot survive underwater—they need oxygen from the air.

Materials

- sharp knife
- empty soda/soft drink bottle with the lid on
- soil
- dead leaves
- pill bugs (either found outside or from a pet store)
- plastic cling wrap
- tape
- small bits of fruits and vegetables
- spray bottle

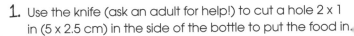

Steps

1. Use the knife (ask an adult for help!) to cut a hole 2 x 1 in (5 x 2.5 cm) in the side of the bottle to put the food in.
2. Fill the bottom of the bottle with a 1-in (2.5-cm) layer of soil. Add a few dead leaves.
3. Lay the bottle on its side, with the cut hole on top, and put a few pill bugs into the bottle.
4. Cover the hole with plastic wrap and tape it in place when you're not feeding them. Poke a few tiny holes in the bottle for air flow. Make sure they're too small for the bugs to get through.
5. Give the pill bugs small pieces of food daily. Which do they like the most? Every couple of days, spritz some water into the "palace" with a spray bottle, keeping the bugs moist.

202 PICK-A-
TRICK

Think you can trick an ant?
Give it a try!

WHAT'S THE SCIENCE?

Ants are excellent navigators. They know where they are at all times, and how to get back to their anthills. Scientists believe that different kinds of ants use either weak signals from Earth's magnetic field, their antennae, and/or the movement of the sun to navigate. Ants always know where they are, which turns they have taken, and how to get back home. In this experiment, the ants are also using their sense of smell to find their way.

Materials

- honey or syrup
- jar lids
- cookies
- other food items of your choice

Steps

1. Go outside and look for ants. Watch their paths. Do they appear to be moving back and forth between two spots (possibly an anthill and a source of food)?

2. Put some honey or syrup on the lid of a jar.

3. Set the jar lid on the ground somewhere that is "off" the ants' path. How do the ants respond to it? Time how long it takes them to find it.

4. Put some crushed cookies onto another jar lid. Set it somewhere else nearby.

5. Observe the ants. How quickly do they find the cookies? Do they appear to be bringing cookie bits home to their anthill? Repeat with other food items of your choice.

6. Continue moving the lids around to different places. If you can, challenge the ants— try setting the lids on top of small hills, or placing sticks and rocks in their paths.

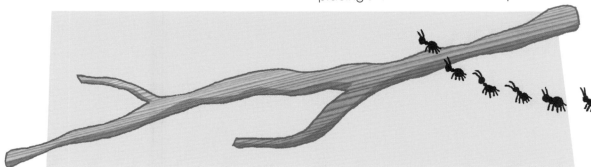

DID YOU KNOW?

When compared to other insects of the same size, ants have the largest brain of all!

203 COLONY, SWEET COLONY

Follow your nose, because it ALWAYS knows!

WHAT'S THE SCIENCE?

Ants in a colony have different roles. Worker ants (who are all female) scout for food. When they find it, they return to the nest, leaving a trail of **pheromones**. Other worker ants follow the scent—adding more pheromones to the trail—and carry the food back to the nest. The queen is the only ant who can lay eggs, so she keeps the species alive. The male ants mate with the queen; they don't work and their life spans are short. Worker ants also dig and maintain the colony and fight off **predators**.

DID YOU KNOW?

*An ant's **abdomen** contains two stomachs. One holds food that the ant will eat, and the other holds food to be shared with others!*

Materials

- rubber gloves
- glass jar
- soil
- water
- leaves
- aluminum foil
- sticky tape
- honey
- spoon
- old stocking
- rubber band
- fresh fruit

> MMM...IS THAT APPLE PIE? MY FAVORITE!

Steps

1. Wearing the rubber gloves, fill the jar with soil. Lightly water the soil, then place the leaves on top.

2. Wrap the foil around the outside of the jar and tape it in place.

3. Put some honey on the spoon and take it outside, along with the jar. Put the spoon on the ground near some ants. When you have ants on the spoon, gently tap it on the jar so that the ants and honey fall on top of the leaves.

4. Place the old stocking over the top of the jar and secure it in place with the rubber band.

5. Keep your ant colony in a cool place, away from the sun.

6. Feed the ants each day with fresh fruit and leaves. Make sure the soil is damp.

7. After a few days, remove the foil and look at the jar. You will see that the ants have made winding tunnels through the soil.

CASTING A SPELL

204

Turn soil into super soil by letting some worms loose in it!

WHAT'S THE SCIENCE?

Earthworms make tunnels by eating the dirt in front of them. The soil then passes out of the worm, along with mucus. This worm waste mixes with dirt to form clumps called castings. Castings make good fertilizers. Many people feed worms their fruit and vegetable scraps and then use the worm castings to fertilize their plants.

Materials

- pebbles
- empty mayonnaise jar
- soil
- a few earthworms (either from the garden or a pet or fishing supply store)
- food scraps (such as fruits, vegetables, coffee grounds, eggshells)
- spray bottle of water
- magnifying glass

Steps

1. Put some pebbles in the bottom of the jar, then add a layer of soil, about 3–5 in (7.5–12.5 cm) deep.
2. Place the worms in the jar.
3. Give the worms some food scraps. Cover the scraps with more soil.
4. Spray water into the jar and give the worms more food scraps daily.
5. Observe the worms as they make tunnels in their new home. Also watch as they eat— and recycle—your leftover food!

NIGHT SIGHT

205

Just like people, different insects have different preferences!

WHAT'S THE SCIENCE?

Different insects like different environments. Some insects, such as moths, prefer light areas. These insects have "positive **phototaxis**" and are attracted to light. Insects that have "negative phototaxis," such as cockroaches, tend to prefer dark areas and are repelled by light.

Materials

- acetate sheet
- ruler
- tape
- scissors
- mesh
- dark paper
- insects (such as crickets, flies, beetles, worms)

Steps

1. Roll the acetate into a tube with a diameter of about 3 in (7.5 cm). Secure the tube with tape.
2. Using the scissors, cut two pieces of mesh to the size of the tube's end. Tape one piece over one end of the tube.
3. Wrap a piece of dark paper around half of the tube and tape it in place.
4. Collect some insects and put them inside the tube.
5. Tape the second mesh piece over the open end of the tube, then lay the tube on its side.
6. Check the tube every half hour or so. How many insects are in the dark side of the tube? How many are in the light side?

206 INSECT IMAGINATION

Insects bugging you?
Design your own!

WHAT'S THE SCIENCE?

Insects are usually small and have wings. They have **exoskeletons** that protect their bodies and support their muscles. Their bodies are divided into three parts: the head, **thorax**, and abdomen. Their antennae, feet, and legs have touch receptors. Insects' diets vary greatly; they may eat bark, flower pollen, fruits, leaves, plant roots, seeds—occasionally even other insects!

Materials

- old boxes and containers of various sizes
- sticky tape
- newspaper
- paint and paintbrush
- markers
- decorations, such as buttons, pipe-cleaners, popsicle/icy pole sticks
- glue

Steps

1. Think of all the things you know about insects, such as their body parts, the colors they use for camouflage, and the number of legs they have. Now design your own insect!

2. Stick the boxes and containers together with the sticky tape to create the body and head.

3. Spread the newspaper on the floor and paint your insect.

4. Leave the paint to dry and then decorate the insect using the markers and other decorations.

207 LEAF LOVERS

Say bon appetit to your bugs!

WHAT'S THE SCIENCE?

Insects are a bit like people—we don't all like the same foods and neither do they. Different kinds of insects eat different kinds of leaves. Flea beetles prefer leafy vegetables and radishes. Millipedes feed on potato tubers, seedlings, and strawberry fruits. Slugs and snails can often be found eating climbing plants and potatoes.

Materials

- 3 small jars
- 3 different insects
- different kinds of leaves (3 of each kind)
- cling wrap
- 3 rubber bands

Steps

1. Collect three different kinds of insects. Place one insect in each jar, along with one of the leaves (use the same kind of leaf in each jar).

2. Cover the jars with cling wrap and secure with a rubber band. Make sure there are small holes in the cover so that the insects can breathe.

3. Leave the jars for a few hours. Which of the insects are eating their leaf?

4. Change the leaves over. Keep repeating the experiment until you have tried all the leaves. Do all the insects like the same kind of leaf?

208 MOTH MAGNETS

Help a moth satisfy its sweet tooth!

Materials

- sugar
- mixing bowl
- warm water
- spoon
- piece of ripe fruit—apricot, peach, or plum
- fork

WHAT'S THE SCIENCE?

Moths eat nectar from flowers and sugar from sap or overripe fruit. A moth looking for food uses its sense of smell. When the right chemical combinations are detected in the air, a moth will fly towards the source and stick out its tongue, searching for nectar. In this experiment, moths are attracted to both the sugar and the aroma of ripe fruit.

Steps

1. Pour some sugar into a bowl.
2. Add a little warm water and stir until most of the sugar has dissolved.
3. Add the fruit and mash it into the mixture with a fork.
4. Go outside and rub the mixture onto some trees.
5. Wait until it is dark, then go outside and look at the places where you put the mixture.

209 WINGED WONDERS

Spot the difference between a butterfly and a moth!

WHAT'S THE SCIENCE?

Butterfly antennae have a tiny ball at the end, which almost looks like a cotton bud when viewed through a magnifying glass. Moths have straight antennae, some with little feathers.

Materials

- butterflies and moths
- bug catcher
- magnifying glass

Steps

1. Catch some moths and butterflies. You might like to use the mixture you made in experiment #208 to attract moths.
2. Decide which of the insects you caught are moths, and which are butterflies. Don't assume that just because it has colorful wings, it is a butterfly!
3. Use a magnifying glass to look carefully at their antennae. What do you see?

210 ON STAGE

"Make" the four stages of a butterfly's life—and then set them out on display!

WHAT'S THE SCIENCE?

A butterfly goes through four stages in its life. First, an adult female butterfly lays eggs on a plant. A caterpillar, or larva, hatches from the egg. It will eat a lot of food as it grows, shedding its skin several times in the process. Next, the caterpillar will stop eating and turn into a **pupa**, or chrysalis, wrapped inside a cocoon. A pupa will remain in its cocoon for at least two weeks, while it grows legs and wings. Finally, the pupa will emerge as a butterfly—and the cycle starts all over again.

Materials

- scissors
- empty egg carton
- glue
- pompoms
- googly eyes
- cardboard tube
- black paint
- paintbrush
- thick paper
- markers
- decorations (glitter, sequins, pipe cleaners}

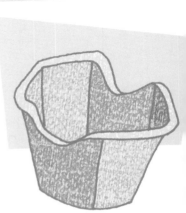

steps

1. Using the scissors, cut an egg nest from the egg carton. This represents the egg the caterpillar hatches from.

2. Glue together several pompoms in a row, forming a caterpillar. If you have googly eyes, glue some onto the first pompom.

3. Paint the cardboard tube black, to look like a cocoon.

4. Draw a butterfly on the thick paper and cut it out. Decorate it with glitter and sequins, and bend and glue on pipe cleaners for antennae.

5. Display the four stages of the butterfly life cycle.

DID YOU KNOW?

The process of a caterpillar becoming a butterfly is called **"metamorphosis."**

211 BEAUTIFUL BUTTERFLIES

Materials

- rubber gloves
- large pot
- soil
- small flowering plants, such as pansies
- watering can

Steps

1. Wearing the rubber gloves, fill the pot with soil until it almost reaches the top.

2. Plant the flowering plants in the pot, leaving space between each plant so they can grow. Make sure that all the roots are covered with soil.

3. Water the plants, then place the pot outside in a sunny spot. Keep watering it regularly. The flowers will attract beautiful butterflies.

Attract butterflies with flowers— and watch them sip sweet nectar!

WHAT'S THE SCIENCE?

Butterflies are attracted to flowers because they feed off them. They are attracted by the nectar of the plant, which you can see them drinking. The nectar of these flowers tastes very sweet to the butterflies.

212 MAGICAL METAMORPHOSIS

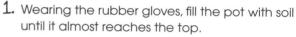

Materials

- water
- small glass jar
- branches with leaves on them
- glass aquarium with a glass lid
- caterpillars found on collected leaves

Steps

1. Pour about ½ inch (1.25 cm) of water into the jar and place the leafy branches in the jar. Put it inside the aquarium and keep it filled at this level.

2. Place the caterpillars on the leaves.

3. Put the lid on securely. The experiment will take several weeks to complete. Replace the leaves regularly as they are eaten, using fresh branches from the same plant. When the caterpillars become fat they will make their cocoons. The cocoons will begin to move when the butterflies are ready to come out.

4. When the butterflies hatch, take the lid off the aquarium so that they can fly free.

Witness the life cycle of a butterfly!

WHAT'S THE SCIENCE?

There are four stages in a butterfly's metamorphosis. 1) It begins life as an egg, which hatches. 2) When it becomes a larva (caterpillar), it hatches from the egg. It begins eating immediately. The larva loses its skin (as it molts) several times.
3) The caterpillar enters the pupa stage by shedding its last layer of soft skin, under which is a hard layer called a chrysalis.
4) After anything from two weeks to several months (depending on the species), a winged butterfly emerges from the chrysalis.

SILKY STUFF

213

Introducing the fussiest eater of all time—the silkworm!

WHAT'S THE SCIENCE?

Most moths form cocoons, but a silkworm's cocoon is formed with a single long thread made from "saliva." A larva hatches from a small, black egg. It feeds on mulberry leaves for one to two months. When the larva is ready to "pupate," it spends three or more days spinning a silk cocoon around itself. In just under a month an adult moth, which cannot fly, emerges from the pupa. Before it dies it will reproduce, laying up to 500 eggs in five days! Silkworms are prized for the silk fiber that comes from the cocoons.

Materials

- scissors
- shoebox with a lid
- silkworms (available online or in insect supply stores)
- mulberry leaves (don't use any other kind— silkworms are very fussy eaters and will starve if you don't use mulberry leaves!)

Steps

1. Using scissors, poke small holes in the lid of the shoebox. Don't make them too big or the silkworms will crawl out!
2. Put the silkworms and mulberry leaves inside the shoebox, then put the lid on the box.
3. Leave the silkworms for a few weeks. Make sure you replace the mulberry leaves regularly.

MELLOW YELLOW

214

Imagine if YOUR mouth were filled with lots of tiny tongues and a thousand teeth!

WHAT'S THE SCIENCE?

Snails have radulas in their mouths, which are hard bands that look like little tongues. On the radulas are rows of teeth. But snails don't actually chew their food, they grind and tear at it with their radulas. Some snails have just a few teeth; others have more than a thousand!

Materials

- snail (from outdoors or from a pet supply store)
- tank or large glass container
- bark
- plant parts
- plastic cling wrap
- pencil or sharp knife (to poke holes)
- banana peel
- magnifying glass

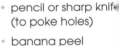

Steps

1. Put the snail in the tank, then add some of the snail's favorite foods, such as bark and plants (both dying and living).
2. Cover the top of the container with cling wrap. Poke holes in the cling wrap using the pencil or knife. Observe the snail as it eats.
3. After a few days, treat the snail to a banana peel. Use a magnifying glass to watch closely as it eats. Can you see its radulas and teeth?

215 SLOW AND STEADY

Have a snail race!

WHAT'S THE SCIENCE?

Snails move around by contracting and relaxing their foot in a sort of wave motion. A snail's foot is a long, flat muscular organ. Snails release a slippery slime as they move, coating the ground beneath them. This helps them to move.

Materials

- small stone
- one or more snails
- watch or stopwatch
- measuring tape
- pen and paper
- calculator

DID YOU KNOW?

A snail may have one or two pairs of tentacles, depending on what type it is. Its eyes may be at the base of its tentacles or at the tips!

Steps

1. Place the stone on the ground. This marks where the snail starts from.
2. Put the snail next to the stone and start the stopwatch.
3. After two minutes, use the measuring tape to measure how far from the stone the snail has traveled. Record the result.
4. Using the calculator, multiply this measurement by 30 to find out how fast the snail moves per hour.
5. If you have more than one snail, you may like to repeat the experiment and compare them. Are some snails faster than others?

216 SUPER STRENGTH

Who would have guessed that snails are super strong?!

WHAT'S THE SCIENCE?

Snails are surprisingly strong animals. When crawling up a vertical surface, they can pull up to 10 times their own weight. When moving horizontally, they can carry about 50 times their own weight!

Materials

- scissors
- empty matchbox tray
- 6-in (15-cm) length of cotton
- one or more snails
- small stones

Steps

1. Using the scissors, poke a small hole in each side of the matchbox tray.
2. Thread one end of the cotton through the holes and tie the ends together to make a loop.
3. Carefully loop the cotton over the snail's shell so the matchbox is behind the snail. See if the snail can pull the matchbox.
4. Now add stones to the matchbox, one at a time. See how many the snail can pull.

217 WIGGLE WONDERS

Read on and find out where to find some wiggly worms!

WHAT'S THE SCIENCE?

There are many species of worms, including bootlace worms, bristle worms, earthworms, flatworms, and roundworms. Worms often live in a damp, dark environment. This is why most worms live underground. Although worms like moisture, the ice in this experiment is much too cold for them.

Materials

- table
- newspaper
- worms in a container of soil
- flashlight/torch
- dry soil
- ice cube

Steps

1. Spread the newspaper out on a table and tip the worms out onto it.
2. Shine the flashlight/torch on them and see how they respond. Now put them on the dry soil and see what happens. Finally, place them on top of the ice cube.
3. When you have finished, put the worms and the soil back into the container and watch the worms burrow down into the soil.

218 GOING BATTY

Some animals "see" using their sense of sound!

WHAT'S THE SCIENCE?

Bats are nocturnal animals. They use **echolocation** to find their way around at night. They send out signals that bounce off objects. They can then work out where an object is by how quickly and clearly the sound bounces back. Bats can even use echolocation to find small insects in mid-air! Bats' ears are shaped to pick up vibrations. The outer part of the ear (called the pinna) is large and curved to collect more of the vibrations in the air.

Materials

- 4–5 friends or family members
- blindfold
- construction paper
- scissors
- markers

Steps

1. Ask one person to stand blindfolded in the middle of the room.
2. Have everyone else spread out around the room.
3. Ask each person in turn to make small, short sounds, such as snaps or whistles. Can the blindfolded person locate the sound? Can they guess how far away it was?
4. Now create a pair of bat ears from construction paper, using the template on this page.
5. Have the blindfolded person hold the bat ears to their ears and try the test again. Could they hear better?

DID YOU KNOW?

A dolphin's head has a large fat deposit, called a melon, which can focus sound, similar to the way the lens of an eye focuses light and allows us to see.

219

BEAST BOX

Count the critters!

WHAT'S THE SCIENCE?

The creatures inside the square will be different depending on what is near the area. If the square is close to a river, or in the shade, or near a big tree, the living things in it will be different from those in the middle of a sunny, grassy area. On a larger scale, animals in different climates adapt differently to their environments. For example, animals in cold wet areas may be able to **insulate** heat while those in dry hot areas may be able to retain water.

Materials

- yard (meter) ruler
- small sticks
- string
- magnifying glass
- notebook and pencil

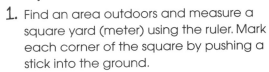

Steps

1. Find an area outdoors and measure a square yard (meter) using the ruler. Mark each corner of the square by pushing a stick into the ground.

2. Tie the string to each of the sticks in turn so it forms a boundary around the square.

3. Sit outside the square and use the magnifying glass to observe the mini-beasts inside the square. Write down what you see.

4. Create another square somewhere else and compare the creatures. Are they different?

220

TADPOLE TIPS

Have fun watching tadpoles grow into frogs!

WHAT'S THE SCIENCE?

Baby frogs begin life as tadpoles with long tails, fins, and gills that filter oxygen from liquid water. Their bodies gradually change as they grow into frogs: they lose their tails, start to grow legs, and develop enclosed lungs that gather oxygen from the air. Soon they will be able to jump! Both types of breathing bring oxygen to the body's **circulatory system**, which carries it to the body's cells.

Materials

- pond water and some pond plants. (Get permission first! Don't use water from the tap.)
- tadpoles (you can get these at a pond or pet store)
- large clear plastic container or aquarium with cover
- large sticks
- lettuce

Steps

1. Pour the pond water and the tadpoles into the container. Add the pond plants. Place the sticks in the container so that they lean against the side and poke out of the water but not over the top of the container (so the frogs have somewhere to sit).

2. Cover the top of the container, leaving a small space so the tadpoles can breathe.

3. Add lettuce leaves each day for food. Remove any uneaten leaves so they do not rot and cause water quality problems. Watch the tadpoles over the following weeks as they change into frogs.

4. Return the frogs to the same pond.

221 PRETTY POND

Make your very own pond—indoors!

WHAT'S THE SCIENCE?

There are many kinds of **microorganisms** in a pond. In freshwater ponds you can find many varieties, such as green algae, amoebas, and diatoms. Each has unique features and plays an important role in the pond ecosystem. Some, such as algae, are autotrophs that make their own food and some, such as amoebas, are heterotrophs that eat other microorganisms.

Materials

- pond water, mud, and plants. (Get permission first!)
- large jar with a lid
- plastic bottle
- stick, slightly shorter than the jar
- magnifying glass

Steps

1. Put some of the mud in the bottom of your jar.
2. Carefully take some small pond plants and plant them in the mud.
3. Half fill the bottle with water from the pond. Pour it into the jar, letting it run down the inside wall.
4. Place the stick in the jar and replace the lid.
5. Leave your "pond" in a shady place and add water if you notice it drying up.
6. Use your magnifying glass to observe what is growing and moving inside the jar. Can you identify some of the living things?

222 GO FISH!

How friendly are your fish?

WHAT'S THE SCIENCE?

There are nearly 30 000 different kinds of fish. Some are microscopic while others are massive. Some live in deep oceans while others prefer shallow waters. Some eat other animals; some only eat plants. But all fish have certain qualities in common. They are all cold-blooded and have fins. They have backbones, meaning they are **vertebrates**. And they pass oxygenated water over their gills in order to "breathe."

Materials

- aquarium full of fish
- notepaper and pen

Steps

1. Think about typical human behavior. What do you like to do during the day? How often do you eat? How often do you talk to other people?
2. Observe the fish in the aquarium for 15-minute intervals throughout the day. Take notes on their behavior in the morning, midday, and at nighttime. Do some fish seem more social than others? Do some seem to prefer time alone?
3. Look in a reference book or online to see what those kinds of fish usually like to do. Do your observations match up?

223 BIRD BUFFET

You're cordially invited—to a bird buffet!

WHAT'S THE SCIENCE?

Different birds have different beaks, shaped to suit the food they eat. Seed-eaters such as sparrows have cone-shaped beaks for cracking seeds. Birds of prey often have "shredder" beaks, with a curved shape that helps them to tear meat apart. "Chisel" beaks, which are long and bore well into wood, can be found on insect-eating woodpeckers. Hummingbirds have "probe" beaks for extracting nectar from flowers.

Materials
- pencil and paper

Steps
1. Sit in your backyard or park and watch the birds.
2. Observe how they eat. For example, some birds will open their beaks first. Others will stick their beaks into the food.
3. Draw a beak on your paper and write how a bird with that kind of beak eats. List the kind of food the bird eats, too.

224 BEST BIRDBATH

Find out which birds are picky eaters—and which aren't!

Materials
- permanent markers
- large plastic container (this will be your birdbath)
- water
- stale bread crusts

Steps
1. Use the markers to decorate your container. Draw flowers and insects so that your birdbath will look pretty in the yard.
2. Fill the container with water.
3. Put some small pieces of bread in the water. This will give the birds something to eat.
4. Place the container outside, in a tree if you can (ask an adult for help). Wait and see who visits!

WHAT'S THE SCIENCE?

Different birds have different diets. Some, such as woodpeckers and warblers, eat insects. Birds of prey, such as owls and hawks, mostly feed on meat. Water-dwelling birds, such as herons and kingfishers, use their long pointy beaks to spear fish. Crows eat almost anything—fruit, insects, fish, even other animals! Just like people, birds need water for both drinking and bathing. It is especially important for birds to keep their feathers bathed and in good condition in cold weather. Well-maintained feathers provide better insulation between the outside air and a bird's skin.

225

BIRD BOOK

This experiment is for the birds!

Materials

- notebook and pencil
- digital camera
- guidebook on birds (try your local library)
- scrapbook
- glue

Steps

1. Sit outside and observe the birds. Make notes about them—their appearance and size, what they are eating, whether they fly, hop, or run. All these things will help you identify the birds.
2. Take photographs of the birds.
3. Print your photos and match them to your notes. Use your guidebook to identify the birds you saw.
4. Glue the photos into your scrapbook and label each kind of bird.

WHAT'S THE SCIENCE?

Birds not only look different, they also behave differently and can do different things. Storks communicate by clapping their **mandibles** together. Hummingbirds weave their nests out of spider webs. They can also fly backward! Birds that fly the fastest in "level flight" (in a straight line not swooping up and down) are ducks and geese. Many sea birds, such as gulls, have red oil droplets in their retinas to filter sunlight.

226

TWEET SUITE

You've heard birds call—but what are they saying?

Materials

- small audio recorder
- notebook and pencil
- a friend

Steps

1. Take the tape recorder outside and record the bird sounds you hear. Remember to be still while listening for their calls—birds have sensitive hearing and may remain quiet if you disturb them.
2. Make notes about any birds you know. This will help you remember which birds were making the sounds.
3. Play the sounds to a friend and see if they recognize the sounds of any birds. It can be quite tricky.

WHAT'S THE SCIENCE?

Birds sing and call to one another for different purposes: to warn of predators; to announce the discovery of a food source; to declare ownership of a territory; and/or to impress potential mates. It can be difficult for us to ascertain the meaning of a bird's calls without special recording equipment, as they can sound quite similar to one another, and in different circumstances they may have different meanings. Most kinds of birds have somewhere between 5 and 15 distinct calls that are recognizable to **ornithologists**.

227

CALL ME

Attract birds with your own sweet songs!

WHAT'S THE SCIENCE?

A human has one voice box, called a larynx. Our larynx makes it possible for us to sing and talk. Birds have a syrinx, which is made up of two voice boxes. Having two voice boxes means birds can make more than one sound at a time, but also makes it is very hard for humans to imitate bird calls accurately!

Materials

- drinking straw
- scissors

Steps

1. Flatten one end of the drinking straw.
2. Using the scissors, cut the flattened end into a point. Make sure it is very flat.
3. Put the flat, pointed end in your mouth and blow hard. This should make a funny noise.
4. You may notice birds looking at you and wondering what type of bird you are!

228

SURFACE SKIMMERS

Some insects can walk on water!

WHAT'S THE SCIENCE?

Water is made of small parts called molecules. The molecules are attracted to each other—some more than others. Water has high surface tension, which means that the molecules at the surface are highly attracted to each other, so the water forms a sort of "skin." Some animals take advantage of this surface tension, walking on top of it without sinking. As they move, their feet make dents in the water's "skin"—but not deep enough to break through it. In this experiment, the attraction between the water molecules will be so strong that they will form balls that will roll over your hand.

Materials

- cooking oil

Steps

1. Sprinkle a few drops of cooking oil onto one of your hands. Rub the drops around.
2. Turn on your sink faucet/tap. Run water over the oily hand. Then turn off the water. What do you notice?

229 CRITTER CHECK

Check in on a wet and wiggly world!

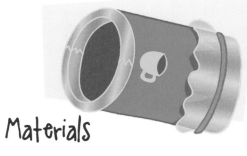

Materials

- can opener
- empty coffee can
- thick tape
- clear plastic wrap
- rubber band
- scissors

Steps

1. Use the can opener to carefully remove both ends from the can.
2. Cover the cut edges with thick tape to be sure that they can't cut you.
3. Cut a piece of plastic wrap to cover one end of the can, allowing for a bit extra to wrap around the edge.
4. Secure the wrap in place with a rubber band. Trim the excess wrap.
5. Test your Critter Checker by placing the wrap-covered edge face down into a bowl of water.
6. Now take your Critter Checker to a nearby pond to see what you can see under the water!

WHAT'S THE SCIENCE?

Ponds are home to many different kinds of animals. Some live in the water, some above it, and others nearby. Depending on where you live you might see any of these small critters with your new scope: amphibians such as frogs, newts, salamanders, and toads; invertebrates such as beetles, leeches, crayfish, and shrimp; fish; or reptiles such as snakes and turtles.

DID YOU KNOW?

Reptiles lay their hard-shelled eggs on land. But many reptiles also spend time in the water.

She did it!

ISOBEL BENNETT

Dr. Isobel Bennett was just 16 years old when her parents enrolled her in a business college. Eight years later, Isobel went to work for the Zoology Department at the University of Sydney. There, Isobel wore many hats including librarian, research assistant, and secretary. Soon, Isobel was regularly visiting and taking students to research stations on Australia's Heron Island and Lizard Island. Isobel went on to write ten books on the Great Barrier Reef and the marine life within it she so adored.

230

BEST BEAKS

Feed on some of these bird beak fun facts!

WHAT'S THE SCIENCE?

The hardness or softness of a bird's beak usually indicates the kind of food they eat. Birds with soft beaks often eat softer foods, such as berries, fruits, and insects (and some seeds). Hard-beaked birds eat tougher foods, such as meat and hard-to-shell seeds. Birds with soft beaks usually swallow their food whole while those with hard beaks chew it first.

Materials

- implements to use as a beak, such as kitchen tongs, tweezers, scissors, pegs, toothpicks, a spoon, and a small strainer
- small pieces of food, such as nuts in shells, uncooked rice, marshmallows, cubes of cheese and gummy worm or snake candies.

Steps

1. Go into the backyard or to the park to do this experiment. Take the implements to use as a beak with you, along with the small pieces of food.
2. Using each of the implements, see what things you can pick up. Try picking up the small pieces of food you've brought with you, along with other items you might find, such as seeds, leaves, soft berries (do not eat them), dirt clumps, twigs, and moss.
3. Try to crack or break the seeds and berries with each "beak." See if you can dig with them.
4. Make a list of the things you were able to pick up with each "beak." Which "beaks" can crack or break each different type of item or dig most effectively?

231

HEAR, PUPPY!

Listen up! Dogs have awesome hearing!

WHAT'S THE SCIENCE?

Dogs have excellent hearing. They can hear sounds before people can, and can sometimes hear sounds that humans can't hear at all. That is why people use guard dogs to protect them. Dogs can wiggle their ears and move them in different directions, which help them to focus on particular sounds.

Materials

- blindfold
- partner or group of people

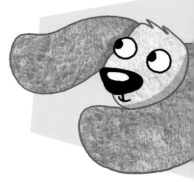

Steps

1. Secure the blindfold over your eyes.
2. Have your partner or the people you are playing with hide around the room.
3. Each person must make a small sound to help you find them. They can also move around the room as you get closer to them. See if you can catch each person.
4. Try playing again, but this time, the people who are hiding don't make any sounds. See if you can hear them walking!

232 HOW TASTY!

Take a journey through five different tastes!

WHAT'S THE SCIENCE?

Your tongue is your body's primary taste organ. It is covered in thousands of tiny taste buds. Taste buds tell you if a food or drink is bitter, salty, sour, or sweet, or savory (also known as 'umami', meaning delicious taste). Umami was only recently recognized as a taste and is found in meats, seafood, vegetables, and dairy foods. It is described as a satisfying, savory, rich, meaty taste that interacts well with the other tastes. Hard cheeses (like Parmesan), cured meats and Asian fish sauces are examples of umami foods.

DID YOU KNOW?

Rabbits have about twice as many taste buds as people. Birds do not have many taste buds—maybe that is why they are not picky eaters. Snakes and crocodiles do not taste food with their tongues. They taste with the roof, or top, of their mouths. Many fish taste food with their mouths and fins. Some fish can even taste with their tails!

Materials

- 5 cups
- water (6 tablespoons per cup)
- ¼ teaspoon sugar
- spoon
- pen or pencil
- sticky labels
- ¼ teaspoon salt
- ¼ teaspoon vinegar
- ¼ teaspoon lemon juice
- ¼ teaspoon brewed tea
- tissues
- soy sauce (low-salt if possible) (ask an adult to assist you with making tea as it uses hot water)
- friend or family member
- eye dropper

Steps

1. Fill one of the cups with water, then add the sugar and stir to dissolve. Label the cup "sweet."
2. Fill the second cup with water, then add the salt and stir to dissolve. Label the cup "salty."
3. Mix the vinegar and lemon juice in the third cup. Label it "sour."
4. Pour the tea into the fourth cup and label it "bitter."
5. Ask a friend or family member to stick out their tongue. Dry it with a tissue.
6. Fill the fifth cup with water and add a few drops of soy sauce. Label it "savory" or "umami."
7. Using the eye dropper, put drops of each mixture, one kind at a time, on the person's tongue. Have the person rinse their mouth with water between taste tests.
8. Can the person recognize all the tastes?

233 WOOF WATCHING

What kinds of tastes do dogs prefer?

WHAT'S THE SCIENCE?

Just like humans, a dog's sense of taste is closely linked to its sense of smell. A dog's taste buds are concentrated around the tip of its tongue. While dogs are familiar with the same tastes we are—bitter, salty, sour, sweet, and savory—their sense of taste is not as strong as ours. In fact, a dog only has one-sixth the number of taste buds that we do!

Materials

- dog
- different kinds of foods (bitter, salty, sour, sweet, and savory)—make sure they are safe for dogs to eat!

Steps

1. Draw up a chart with rows and columns. In the rows, list the times when you feed your dog. In each column, list the foods you will test. Each day, be sure to test one food for each taste group—bitter, salty, sour, sweet, and savory.

2. Observe the dog's reaction to each kind of food, and note it on the chart.

3. At the end of the week, check the results. Which taste had the most positive response?

4. If you can, test more than one dog and compare your data!

234 SMELL TO TELL

No wonder sharks make such excellent predators!

WHAT'S THE SCIENCE?

Sharks have an amazing sense of smell that helps them hunt their prey. A shark has a pair of nostrils under its snout through which water and **olfactory** information constantly flow. The shark's nostrils are not used for breathing; their primary function is to communicate smells to the shark's brain. Even the glass marked "1 drop" is still 50 times the minimum a shark could smell.

Materials

- 3 large drinking glasses
- sticky labels
- marker
- measuring jug
- water
- perfume or essential oil, such as lavender

Steps

1. Label the glasses "10 drops," "5 drops," and "1 drop."

2. Fill each glass with 2 cups of water.

3. In the glass marked "10 drops," place 10 drops of perfume. Repeat with the other glasses, using 5 drops and 1 drop.

4. Swirl each glass around carefully to mix the water and the perfume.

5. Now smell each glass. Which has the strongest smell?

235 THAT'S RIGHT!

This experiment is pawsitively fun!

WHAT'S THE SCIENCE?

Most people are left- or right-handed, depending on how their brains work. Until recently, scientists didn't believe that animals also had a hand preference. However, they now believe that some animals, including monkeys, may rely more on one hand more than the other for certain tasks.

Materials

- two sheets of paper
- pen or pencil
- cat
- string

Steps

1. On one piece of paper make a table with two columns. Label one column "LEFT" and the other "RIGHT."

2. Closely study the cat's behavior, both indoors and out. Which paw does it use and when? Place a tick in the "left" or "right" column whenever you see it use that paw.

3. Test the cat by "teasing" it with a piece of string. Does it swat at the string with one or both paws?

4. Crumple the other sheet of paper loudly, then throw the paper ball so the cat chases it. Which paw does the cat use to retrieve it?

5. Keep track of when and how frequently the cat uses its left and right paws. Do you think it is left- or right-pawed?

6. If possible, repeat the experiment with another cat.

DID YOU KNOW?

Cats do not have sweat glands all over their bodies like people do—they sweat through their paws!

236 LOOKING GOOD

How do animals see the world?

WHAT'S THE SCIENCE?

Human eyesight is called "stereoscopic vision." Both eyes see the same object. But because there is a slight distance between the two eyes, each eye sees the object slightly differently. Some animals, such as rabbits, have eyes on the sides of their head. This gives them a wide range of view. Some birds can see 360 degrees—without even turning their heads! Some animals that hunt prey, such as eagles and wolves, rely on **stereopsis** to reduce their field of view and zoom in on their targets.

Materials
- two drinking glasses
- table

Steps

1. Put the glasses in front of you on a table. One should be about 12 in (30 cm) away from you, and the other about 35 in (90 cm) away from you.

2. Rest your chin on the table with both glasses directly ahead of you.

3. Close one of your eyes and look ahead. Then close the other eye and look ahead. What happens when you look at the glasses with one eye instead of two?

237 FELINE FOOD

Make this purr-fect treat for your cat!

WHAT'S THE SCIENCE?

Cat grass is actually a plant grown from wheat berry seeds. Domestic cats eat it to help with their **digestion**. The grass provides **roughage** that helps break down hairballs. Wild cats eat other grass-eating animals to get the same kinds of roughage.

Materials
- 2 tablespoons wheat berry seeds
- bowl
- water (room temperature)
- container
- soil
- plastic cling wrap

Steps

1. Put the wheat berry seeds in the bowl and cover them with water. Leave the seeds to soak for seven hours.

2. Fill the container with soil, then sprinkle the wet seeds over the top. Cover the container with cling wrap.

3. Leave the container in a dark room or closet. Make sure the soil stays moist, checking it daily.

4. When the seeds start to sprout, move the container to a sunny spot and remove the cling wrap. Leave it for a week or so, and watch your cat grass grow!

 **238** BLUBBER

BUDDIES

Blubber is like a layer of super-fat!

WHAT'S THE SCIENCE?

Blubber is a thick layer of fatty material in the outer layer of skin in marine mammals such as whales and seals. It acts as a thermal insulator, which keeps an object warm or cool by absorbing or trapping heat. Blubber can be up to 20 in (50 cm) thick in a large whale! It traps heat and keeps the cold water from affecting the animal's inner tissues. In this experiment the shortening acts like a layer of blubber, trapping the heat in the water.

Materials

- water
- two buckets (one small enough to fit into the other)
- thermometer
- softened vegetable shortening or lard
- two large plastic bags

Steps

1. Place warm water in the smaller bucket, then put that bucket into the larger bucket.

2. Fill the larger bucket with very cold water. The cold water should surround the smaller bucket.

3. Using the thermometer, measure the temperature of the water in the small bucket. Check it again every ten minutes. How long does it take to cool down?

4. Do the experiment again, but this time, put the small bucket of warm water in one of the plastic bags. Put the vegetable shortening in the second plastic bag, then sit the small bucket (wrapped in the first bag) inside it.

5. Now, place the small bucket in a large bucket of cold water.

6. Test the temperature of the warm water and see if it changes temperature as quickly as it did the first time!

DID YOU KNOW?

Baby whales are born without much blubber, so the milk they are fed by their mothers is very high in fat.

239 THAT'S A WRAP!

Animals have what it takes to live in extreme environments!

WHAT'S THE SCIENCE?

Animals have different kinds of insulators to help keep them warm or cool in the environment they live in. These insulators can be things such as fur, feathers, or blubber. Some materials trap heat, and others **conduct** it. Birds' feathers have lots of pockets of warm air between them, lying near the skin. These help to keep the birds warm.

DID YOU KNOW?

Scientists studying in the arctic wear outfits with many layers—sometimes up to seven! The layers protect their skin from the extreme arctic temperatures.

Materials

- 4–5 small jars, such as baby food jars
- 4–5 scraps of material, such as denim, foil, felt, or cotton, each big enough to cover the outside of one of the jars
- 4–5 rubber bands
- warm water
- thermometer
- notebook and pen

Steps

1. Cover the outside of each jar with a piece of material, as though you are giving it a coat. Secure the material with a rubber band.

2. Fill each jar with warm water. Using the thermometer, measure the temperature of the water in each jar. Record the temperatures in your notebook.

3. Check the temperature of each jar every 5 minutes for 30 minutes. Which got cold faster? Which material held in the heat?

WONDER WORDS

abdomen—A section of an insect's body, where its digestive organs are located.

amphibians—Vertebrates that are cold-blooded, and spend time in both land and water.

arachnid—A class of arthropods with eight legs and no antennae, which includes spiders, ticks and scorpions.

arthropod—A group of invertebrates with exoskeletons, segmented bodies, and pairs of jointed limbs.

bacteria—Microscopic, single-celled organisms that are critical to our ecosystems and to our bodies. While some can cause disease, others are beneficial, living in soil, water, and the bodies of animals and plants.

birds—Vertebrates that are warm-blooded, lay eggs, and have feathers and wings.

carnivores—Animals that eat meat.

circulatory system—The bodily system that includes the blood, heart, and vessels, which is responsible for the circulation of oxygen and carbon dioxide throughout the body, the delivery of nutrients and other essential materials to cells, and the removal of waste products.

classification—Categorizing organisms based on information such as their evolutionary and structural characteristics.

cold-blooded—Having a body temperature that varies depending on the surrounding environment, rather than being regulated by the body.

conduct— To channel or transmit heat, electricity or sound.

crustaceans—Arthropods with exoskeletons that live in water.

digestion—The process by which the body converts food into substances that it can then absorb and use.

echolocation—Locating objects by sending out sound waves and tracking how long they take to bounce back, and from which direction.

exoskeletons—Hard structures such as shells that protect and support a body.

fish—Vertebrates that are cold-blooded, live and breathe in water, and that typically have fins, gills, and scales.

fungi—Fungi make up their own kingdom of living things. They don't contain chlorophyll and they feed on organic matter.

gills—Organs that aquatic creatures use to take in oxygen from water.

herbivores—Animals that eat plants.

insulate—To prevent electricity, heat, or sound from passing through.

invertebrates—Animals without backbones.

mammals—Vertebrates that are warm-blooded and have skin that is covered in hair. Female mammals typically produce milk to feed to their young.

mandibles—The lower jaws of vertebrates.

marsupials—A group of mammals in which the females have teats for feeding their babies, and pouches on their abdomens for carrying them.

metamorphosis—A change of form, structure, or substance that occurs in some animals as they transform into an adult stage.

microorganisms—Organisms, such as bacterium, that are so small they are only visible through a microscope.

microscopic—So small as to only be visible through a microscope.

monotremes—Mammals that lay eggs.

nocturnal—Active at night.

olfactory—To do with the sense of smell.

ornithologists—Scientists who study birds.

pheromones—Chemical substances produced by animals and used as signals between one another.

phototaxis—The movement of an organism or cell towards or away from light.

phyla—A division of organisms, which is above a class and below a kingdom.

pollination—The process by which pollen is transferred from a flower's anther to its stigma, which often leads to fertilization.

predator—An animal that hunts or catches other animals for food.

prey—An animal hunted or caught for food.

primatologist—A scientist who studies mammals called primates.

proboscis—A long, tube-shaped organ found on certain animals, used for feeding.

protein—A molecule made up of amino acids that are essential for life.

pupa—An insect in the process of metamorphosing, between larva and adult.

reptiles—Vertebrates that are cold-blooded, breathe through lungs, and are covered in scales or horny plates.

retina—The tissue at the back of the eyeball containing light-sensitive cells that pass nerve impulses to the brain which are perceived as a visual image.

roughage—The indigestible elements of food that promote healthy bowel function, such as fiber.

spinnerets—Tubes through which spiders and some insect larvae spin silk threads, often used to form their webs and cocoons.

stereopsis—Vision that combines the images perceived by each eye to form one complete picture.

thorax—A section of an insect's body, located between its head and abdomen.

vertebrates—Animals with backbones.

warm-blooded—Able to maintain a relatively constant and warm body temperature that is not affected by the surrounding environment.

zoologist—A scientist who studies the animal kingdom and animal life.

FUN LAB
CHEMISTRY

240 BASIC BEAUTY

Make new soap from old soap!

Materials

- grater
- leftover pieces of soap (approx. ¼ of a bar)
- saucepan
- 1 to 2 teaspoons of water
- large spoon
- food coloring
- roller and/or shaped cookie cutter

Steps

1. Grate the soap pieces into small flakes.
2. Put the flakes into the saucepan with the water.
3. Stir the mixture on the stove over a low heat until it becomes mushy.
4. Stir in a three drops of food coloring.
5. Turn the heat off and allow the soap to cool a bit. When it is still warm and soft (but not too hot to touch), shape it into a ball, flatten it like a pancake, or use a cookie cutter to give it a special shape!
6. Now leave your soap somewhere cool until it hardens. Once it is set, it's ready to use!

WHAT'S THE SCIENCE?

Some chemical substances have either **acidic** and or **basic** properties. Acids are rich in **hydrogen ions**; bases are poor in hydrogen ions. Acidic liquids tend to taste sour; basic liquids usually taste bitter. When mixed together, acids and bases form salts and water. To make soap, mix a fatty acid with a base (an **alkaline** solution). Liquid soap can be alkaline, or it can be **neutralized**. Solid soap can have some alkaline residue or it can be neutralized while it is processed. Basic substances, such as soap, tend to be effective cleaners.

241 BRIGHT 'N' BUBBLY

Make your very own brand of bubble bath!

WHAT'S THE SCIENCE?

Molecules are groups of two or more **atoms** that are bonded together. Molecules move faster in hot water than in cold water, which is why the food coloring drops spread and dissolve quickly in your bubble bath. If you were to repeat this experiment using cold water, the food coloring would spread much more slowly.

Materials

- cup clear/anti-dandruff shampoo
- ½ cups hot water
- medium-sized bowl
- large spoon
- ½ teaspoon of salt
- food coloring
- large bottle or jar

Steps

1. Mix the shampoo and water together in the bowl.
2. Stir in the salt until the solution has thickened.
3. Stir in a few drops of food coloring.
4. Pour the bubble bath solution into the bottle or jar.

242

pH

PREP

There's more to your soap than just its color or scent!

WHAT'S THE SCIENCE?

Different liquid soaps have different **pH levels**. The pH level measures how many hydrogen, or H+, **ions** the soap contains. Soaps with high pH levels are basic, soaps with low pH levels are acidic, and those with a pH level of 7 are neutral. Indicators can be used to find out if a substance is acidic or basic. The indicator changes color depending on the pH level in the soap.

DID YOU KNOW?

Liquid soaps typically have lower pH levels than bar soaps.

Materials

- one red cabbage
- blender
- water
- medium bowl (microwave-safe)
- small bowl
- two coffee filters
- scissors
- cups
- liquids for testing (detergent, hand soap, witch hazel, aftershave)

Steps

1. Chop the cabbage in the blender, adding a few drops of water if necessary.

2. Transfer the chopped cabbage into the medium bowl and heat it in the microwave on low heat for 20 seconds. Continue to heat for 10 second intervals until you see steam rising from the cabbage.

3. Remove the bowl from the microwave (careful, it will be hot!) and set it aside to cool for 15 minutes.

4. Sit a coffee filter in the small bowl and pour the cabbage into the filter. Allow it to drain. Throw away the cabbage-filled filter.

5. Put a second coffee filter into the liquid left in the bowl and let it soak, then remove the filter and set it aside to dry for one day.

6. Cut the dried filter paper into test strips.

7. Fill small cups with different liquid cleaners.

8. Make a chart showing the pH level of each liquid (you will find this on the label) and the color you see on your tester when you dip it into the liquid.

9. Which colors correspond with the more basic substances, and which with the more acidic?

243 SUDS BUDS

Strawberries and cream for the skin—oh, my!

WHAT'S THE SCIENCE?

Most soaps are made in a chemical reaction that happens when certain fats are mixed with certain bases. This process is called **saponification**. In this experiment you will mix together a basic soap with milk, which is a fat. Soaps that are created through saponification should have a pH level of between 8 and 11.

Materials

- 4-oz (110-g) bar of fragrance-free soap
- grater
- water
- saucepan
- heatproof bowl
- ¼ cup powdered milk
- spoon
- potholders
- red food coloring
- strawberry essential oil
- vanilla extract
- soap or candy mold tray

Steps

1. Grate the soap into small pieces.
2. With an adult's help, boil 2 cups of water in the saucepan on the stove.
3. Place a heatproof bowl on top of the saucepan. Make sure it fits tightly so it cannot move.
4. Mix together the grated soap, powdered milk, and ¼ cup of water in the bowl. Stir often until it has combined into a liquid.
5. Using potholders, remove the bowl and leave it to cool.
6. Once it has cooled, stir in several drops each of food coloring, strawberry essential oil, and vanilla extract.
7. Pour the soap mixture into the soap molds. Leave the soaps for at least one day before removing them.

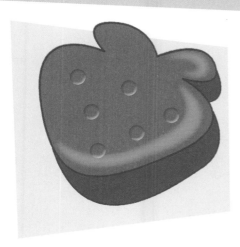

DID YOU KNOW?

Most people's skin has a pH level of between 4.5 and 5.5, which is acidic. Because saponified soaps have a pH level of 8 or higher, they can be quite drying for most skin types.

HOORAY FOR SHEA

244

Skin feeling dry?
Let shea save the day!

WHAT'S THE SCIENCE?

Soaps are traditionally made from **triglycerides**—oils and fats. Sometimes additional fats are also added to provide different **properties**. Shea butter, palm kernel oil, cottonseed oil, cocoa butter, and hemp oils are examples. They help to condition and moisturize skin.

Materials

- 2 cups water
- saucepan
- heatproof bowl
- 4-oz (110-g) shea butter melt-and-pour soap base
- 1 tablespoon finely ground oatmeal
- ½ tablespoon rose petal powder
- red food coloring
- potholders
- rose essential oil
- ylang ylang essential oil
- spoon
- soap or candy mold tray

Steps

1. With an adult's help, boil the water in a saucepan on the stove.
2. Place a heatproof bowl on top of the saucepan. Make sure it fits tightly so it cannot move.
3. Melt the shea butter soap base in the bowl, then add the oatmeal, rose petal powder, and food coloring, stirring often until the mixture is well blended.
4. Use potholders to remove the bowl, then leave it to cool.
5. Stir in several drops of each of the essential oils.
6. Pour the soap mixture into the soap molds. Leave the soaps for at least one full day before removing them.

DID YOU KNOW?

If you use a different type of fat in this recipe instead of shea butter, the soap will look and feel different.

SOOTHE AND SMOOTH

245

Honey-scented bubbles—
what could be more luxurious?

Materials

- 2 tablespoons honey
- 2 tablespoons fresh lemon or grapefruit juice
- 2 tablespoons bubble bath
- small bowl
- spoon
- bathtub
- pH tester (available at most pharmacies or you can use the cabbage juice indicator from experiment 242: pH Prep)

Steps

1. Slowly mix together the honey, juice, and bubble bath in a small bowl.

2. Turn on the hot faucet/tap in the bath, then pour the mixture into the warm water as it fills the bath.

3. When the bath is three-quarters full, turn off the water. Test the water with your pH tester. Is it more acidic or basic?

WHAT'S THE SCIENCE?

Mix this refreshing bath to test your knowledge of acids and bases. Bubble-bath mixtures often have basic properties, as strong alkaline substances are used to create them. Most citrus fruits contain a weak acid called citric acid. When you add them both to water, you could create an acidic, basic, or neutral substance. An indicator detects how much acidity the solution has. Will the alkaline bubble bath overpower the acidic lemon juice? Find out!

MINERAL BATH

246

For hundreds of years, people have used Epsom salts to treat dry, damaged skin!

Materials

- bath
- 1 cup Epsom salts

Steps

1. Start running warm water into the bath. While the water is running, use your hand to mix in the Epsom salts.

2. Sit in the bath for at least 15 minutes to get the full benefits of the Epsom salts.

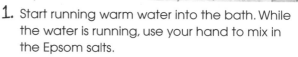

WHAT'S THE SCIENCE?

Epsom salts are not like table salt! They are a mineral **compound** of magnesium and sulfate. Our skin can easily absorb magnesium, and it is good for our health. Magnesium reduces inflammation and helps muscle and nerve function.

DID YOU KNOW?

Sodium chloride is the most common salt. We know it as "table salt."

247 RAINBOW READERS

Make a pH rainbow!

WHAT'S THE SCIENCE?

Scientists use strips of treated paper, called indicators, to determine how basic or acidic a substance is. A color scale is used to show pH values from 0 to 14. The indicators change color depending on the pH value.

Materials

- paper
- ruler
- markers
- crayons or colored pencils

Steps

1. Rule a line on your paper and divide it into 15 equal sections.

2. Using colored pencils, fill in your scale as follows:

   0 Dark red = battery acid

   1 Light red = stomach acid

   2 Pink = lemon juice, vinegar

   3 Orange = orange juice

   4 Peach = tomato juice

   5 Yellow = black coffee

   6 Pale yellow = milk

   7 Green = neutral – fresh water

   8 Light green = baking soda/bicarbonate of soda

   9 Teal = toothpaste

   10 Light blue = **antacid** tablets

   11 Turquoise = ammonia for household cleaning

   12 Medium blue = very soapy water

   13 Navy blue = bleach

   14 Dark blue = drain cleaner or caustic soda

DID YOU KNOW?

Microorganisms can help make a liquid more acidic or basic by producing acids and bases like lactic acid and ammonia.

248 BYE–BYE DRY

Try having your oatmeal in the shower!

WHAT'S THE SCIENCE?

As hot water is mixed with the oatmeal and bran, the water is absorbed and the cereal expands. Water will **evaporate**. As it does, it changes its state from a liquid to gas, and goes into the air.

Materials

- 1½ cups dry oatmeal
- 1½ cups dry bran
- small bowl
- 1⅓ cups hot water
- spoon
- kitchen scales

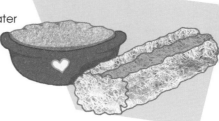

Steps

1. Mix the oatmeal and bran in a small bowl.
2. Slowly add the hot water while stirring the mixture, until the oatmeal and bran are wet but not overly sticky.
3. Weigh the bowl, and then set it aside overnight. Weigh the bowl again in the morning. Does it weigh the same amount?
4. You can use a dollop of this mixture as a scrub in the shower (along with a loofah or washcloth). Scrub for about a minute to get rid of old dead skin.

249 SKIN OF SILK

Give your skin a spring clean with this moisturizing scrub!

WHAT'S THE SCIENCE?

Many oils serve as effective **emollients**, stopping moisture from leaving the skin. This reduces evaporation, so helps increase skin's hydration (water content). In this scrub, the sea salt will rub away dead skin cells, while the oils will hydrate the skin.

Materials

- 3 tablespoons sea salt (for a gentler scrub, use sugar instead of salt)
- 1 tablespoon almond oil
- 1 tablespoon olive oil
- bowl
- spoon
- 1 tablespoon peppermint oil
- small jar or plastic container

*WARNING:
Those with nut allergies may be sensitive to this experiment as it uses almond oil!*

Steps

1. Place the sea salt, almond oil, and olive oil in a bowl and stir until they form a paste.
2. Add three drops of peppermint oil, then stir again.
3. Put the mixture in the jar or container.
4. Use as a body scrub by rubbing it onto your skin, then rinsing off.

250 BATH BOMBS

Add some fizz to your next bath!

WHAT'S THE SCIENCE?

Citric acid is a powerful cleaning agent that is found in many household cleaning products. The citric acid in the bath bombs helps rinse away dirt and grime. The baking soda acts as an abrasive. Together, they fizz as the acid and base react in warm water. The reaction releases carbon dioxide (CO_2), which causes the bubbles you see.

She did it!

Madame CJ Walker
USA

Materials

* ½ cup citric acid powder (also called "sour salt", which is different from regular salt. Available in some pharmacies, health food and vitamin stores, or supermarkets.)
* 1 cup baking soda/bicarbonate of soda
* spoon
* small bowl
* food coloring
* scented oil
* ½ cup witch hazel
* spray bottle
* molds (dome-shaped is best)
* bath

Steps

1. Mix the citric acid and baking soda/bicarbonate of soda together. Make sure they are mixed well, or your bath bomb will be grainy.
2. In a small bowl, mix together a few drops of food coloring and scented oil, then add them to the baking soda and citric acid.
3. Pour the witch hazel into a spray bottle. Spray it into the mixture with one hand while mixing with the other. (This step can be tricky. You may want to ask a friend to help!) The mixture will dry quickly so you need to work fast.
4. When the mixture begins to harden, quickly transfer it into the molds, then leave it to set for an hour.
5. Remove the bath bombs from the molds and leave them out to air dry for another six hours.
6. Now run your bath, add a bath bomb and see what happens!

Madame C J Walker was born as Sarah Breedlove in Louisiana in 1867. Her parents died when she was just six years old, leaving her orphaned. By the age of 20 Sarah had already married, had a baby, and was a widow. Sarah soon noticed she was losing her hair due to a scalp disease, which was common in those days. She developed a product that helped her to regrow her hair. Friends and family members were so impressed by the regrowth that they requested some of the product for themselves. Word spread, and soon Sarah's product, sold under her professional name Madame C J Walker, was being sold nation-wide. Before long she was a millionaire!

251 THE ACID TEST

Lemons might be small, but they're pretty powerful!

WHAT'S THE SCIENCE?

Stick a piece of zinc and a piece of copper into a lemon to draw electrical power from the lemon through an external circuit. The zinc acts as the **anode**. This side of the battery reacts with the citric acid in the lemon to make the zinc negatively charged. This creates negatively charged **electrons** that flow towards the **cathode**, or the copper, which is positively charged. This changes the energy of the chemical reaction into electric energy by creating an electron flow, which is made when electrons are attracted to the positively charged copper and move towards it.

Materials

- 2 lemons
- 2 flat strips of zinc
- 2 flat strips of copper
- pliers
- insulated wire
- 9-volt LED (light emitting diode)

Steps

1. Put a lemon on the table and push a strip of copper into one end and a strip of zinc into the other.
2. Do the same in the other lemon.
3. Using the pliers, cut two 8-in (20-cm) lengths of insulated wire. Take one of the pieces and cut it in half. Trim the plastic insulation from the ends of the wires so that there is some wire visible.
4. Attach the long piece of wire to one of the terminals of the light, and attach the other end to the piece of zinc on one of the lemons.
5. Connect one end of one of the shorter pieces of wire to the copper on the same lemon. Connect the other end to the zinc on the other lemon.
6. Holding the last piece of wire by the insulated section, connect one end to the remaining piece of copper. Connect the other end to the other point on the light bulb.

DID YOU KNOW?

Early Europeans used lemons to sweeten their breath—and to repel moths!

252 COCOA GLOW

Some fats are to be avoided, but these ones are good for you!

WHAT'S THE SCIENCE?

The cocoa butter and almond oil in the moisturizer are both fatty acids. Fatty acids are "building blocks" of fat that we absorb from the foods we eat. Fatty acids help our bodies by storing and producing energy. When applied to our skin, fatty acids reduce swelling and hold in essential moisture.

Materials

- grater
- ¼ cup beeswax
- ¼ cup cocoa butter
- heatproof bowl
- saucepan
- water
- 1 teaspoon almond oil
- potholders
- jar with fitted lid

WARNING:
Those with nut allergies may be sensitive to this experiment as it uses almond oil!

DID YOU KNOW?

Flax seeds, walnuts, shrimp/prawns, tuna, and winter squash/pumpkin are all foods that are high in omega-3 fatty acids. People with diets that are low in fatty acids often have dry, flaky skin.

Steps

1. Grate the beeswax and cocoa butter into the heatproof bowl.
2. Heat 2 cups of water in the saucepan.
3. Set the bowl on top of the saucepan, making sure it fits securely. Stir the beeswax and cocoa butter until they melt.
4. Stir in the almond oil.
5. Use potholders to remove the bowl and set it aside to cool.
6. Pour the cream into a jar and use it whenever your skin needs a deep moisturizing treatment.

253 CHOCO-HEAVEN

Chocolate doesn't just taste good—it feels good, too!

WHAT'S THE SCIENCE?

One of the main ingredients in chocolate is sugar. Sugar is one of the most important molecules for all living things because it provides energy. It is the basic type of **cellular** "food," or fuel. In this experiment, sugar granules act as an exfoliant (something that removes dead skin cells), while cocoa butter acts as a moisturizer.

Materials

- 2 teaspoons chocolate milk
- 1 teaspoon chocolate syrup
- ½ cup honey
- 2 tablespoons brown sugar
- medium-sized bowl
- spoon

Steps

1. Put the chocolate milk, syrup, honey, and brown sugar in the bowl and stir until combined.

2. Smooth a dollop or two onto your skin and rub it in. Enjoy the aroma for as long as you want before rinsing it off!

254 SKIN SCIENCE

Protect your skin from the scorching sun!

WHAT'S THE SCIENCE?

Sunscreen protects our skin from harmful UV rays. The SPF of a sunscreen stands for Sun Protection Factor. A sunscreen's SPF is based on its chemical ability to block different amounts of UV light. When combined, a sunscreen's chemicals absorb high-energy UV rays, then release them as lower-energy rays. This stops the UV rays from reaching your skin and resulting in sunburn and long-term skin problems. The blockers are usually made of zinc oxide or titanium oxide.

Materials

- color-changing material, such as sun-sensitive cloth, sun-paper, or color changing beads
- clear plexiglass or plastic
- 2–3 types of sunscreen, each with a different SPF

Steps

1. In a shady area, put the color-changing material under the clear plexiglass or plastic.

2. Place a dollop of each sunscreen on the plexiglass above the color-changing material. Leave a small area without sunscreen.

3. Move the materials into a sunny area.

4. After 10 minutes, wipe the sunscreen off the plexiglass and study the material underneath. Did the sunscreen make a difference to how much the color changed?

255 FINGER FAVES

Shea butter is the perfect antidote to dry or yellow fingernails!

Materials

- shea butter
- soft cotton gloves

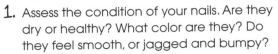

WHAT'S THE SCIENCE?

Shea butter comes from African shea tree nuts. It can be eaten, but is mostly used in creams and ointments. Shea butter is mostly nonsaponifiable, meaning it cannot be converted into soap by alkalis. Shea butter is an effective moisturizer, emollient, and **humectant**. When applied to skin, shea butter melts and is absorbed almost instantly.

Steps

1. Assess the condition of your nails. Are they dry or healthy? What color are they? Do they feel smooth, or jagged and bumpy?
2. Every night for a week, apply shea butter to your nails and cuticles at bedtime, then put on the cotton gloves.
3. Remove the gloves in the morning.
4. At the end of the week, check the condition of your nails. Have they changed?

256 YOU NAILED IT!

Follow these simple steps to brighten your nails!

Materials

- lemon
- small bowl
- soap
- moisturizer
- baking soda/ bicarbonate of soda
- cotton swab

WHAT'S THE SCIENCE?

The scientific name for baking soda is sodium bicarbonate, and its chemical formula is $NaHCO_3$. Baking soda is a **leavening agent**, which is why it is added to baked goods before cooking. It produces carbon dioxide, causing batter to expand and dough to rise. In this experiment, the baking soda acts as an abrasive, which is any type of rough material used to smooth or polish a surface.

Steps

1. Juice the lemon into the bowl. Soak your nails in the juice for five minutes.
2. Wash your hands with soap and then moisturize them.
3. Add some baking soda/bicarbonate of soda to the lemon juice and stir to form a paste. Apply a small amount of the paste to each fingernail.
4. Leave the paste on your nails for five minutes, then rinse it off.

257 CHEMICAL CUPCAKES

Find out how to make your cupcakes bubble!

WHAT'S THE SCIENCE?

When you are baking a cake, acids and bases make the dough "rise." The reaction between an acid (here it is vinegar) and base (here it is baking soda) produces carbon dioxide bubbles that you can actually see in the cakes.

Materials

- ¼ cup sugar
- 1 tablespoon butter
- ¼ teaspoon vanilla essence
- ¼ cup milk
- ⅛ teaspoon salt
- ¾ cup all-purpose flour/plain flour
- large mixing spoon
- ¼ teaspoon baking soda/bicarbonate of soda
- ½ teaspoon white vinegar
- cupcake tray with cupcake liners

Steps

1. Mix the sugar, butter, vanilla, and milk. Add the salt and flour and mix well with a large mixing spoon.
2. Mix in the baking soda/bicarbonate of soda and vinegar. Pour the mix into the cupcake liners.
3. Bake at 375° F (190° C) for 10 minutes, then remove from the oven (ask an adult for help) and set aside to cool.
4. Cut a cupcake in half. Look at the bubbles in the cupcake!

258 SWEET FEET

Pamper your feet at the end of a long day!

WHAT'S THE SCIENCE?

As well as being a leavening and cleaning agent, baking soda also has anti-bacterial powers. It can be added to water to make the water more basic, which makes it a stronger cleaning agent.

Materials

- warm bath water
- 3 cups Epsom salts
- 6 drops of marjoram essential oil (or another aroma if you cannot find marjoram)
- pH indicator
- 1 cup baking soda/bicarbonate of soda

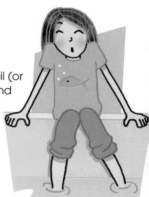

Steps

1. Pour the Epsom salts into the bath and mix them in with your hands.
2. Add the essential oil, then use the pH indicator to test the water's pH level.
3. Mix in half of the baking soda/bicarbonate of soda. Test the pH level again—has it changed?
4. Add the remaining baking soda, then test the pH level again. What happened?
5. Now soak your feet in the bath and relax!

259 COOL AS A CUCUMBER

Grab a few things from the fridge and kiss that oily complexion goodbye!

WHAT'S THE SCIENCE?

Molecules are groups of two or more atoms bonded together. The natural citric acid in lime is powerful enough to break up oil molecules. That's why this recipe works on oily skin—it allows oils to be lifted and rinsed off.

Materials

- 1 cucumber
- peeler
- grater
- 2 cups water
- blender
- coffee filter
- small bowl
- 1 teaspoon lime juice
- washcloth

Steps

1. Peel the cucumber. Set aside the peel for later. Grate the cucumber into small pieces.
2. Pour the water and cucumber into the blender, and puree.
3. Pour the contents of the blender into a coffee filter and strain the cucumber water.
4. Place two teaspoons of the cucumber water in a small bowl and mix in the lime juice.
5. Spread the mixture over your face. Leave it on for half an hour.
6. Wash your face with warm water and a washcloth.
7. Drink the remainder of the cucumber juice for an added glow!

260 GUM BE GONE

Ever had gum stuck in your hair? Here's the solution!

WHAT'S THE SCIENCE?

Chewing gum contains **polymers**—repeating patterns of molecules, which can be stretched when chewed. It also contains softeners and flavorings. To get rid of gum, you have to dissolve it first. Which of these will work best to dissolve the gum?

Materials

- 2–3 small bunches of hair about 2-in (5-cm) long (Don't cut your own hair—ask for hair from a local barber)
- tea towel
- masking tape
- chewed gum
- peanut butter
- rubbing alcohol (never ingest!)
- vegetable oil

WARNING: Those with nut allergies may be sensitive to this experimen[t] as it uses peanut butter!

Steps

1. Lay the bunches of hair out on the tea towel. Tape them down securely.
2. Put some chewing gum on each bunch of hair. Rub it in!
3. Now place a different **solvent**—peanut butter, rubbing alcohol, or vegetable oil—on each bunch of hair. Rub the hair with the solvent, and see if the gum comes out. Which worked best?

261 CLEAN QUEEN

Show your friends you care—about their hair!

Materials

- 3 different kinds of shampoo with different pH levels (check the label to find the pH level)
- two friends, one with curly hair and one with straight hair

Steps

1. Give each friend enough of each shampoo to wash her hair with it for three days (nine days in total).
2. Ask each friend to use each kind of shampoo for three days in a row. Have them record what they notice about their hair each day.
3. Which shampoo did each friend prefer? What do you notice about the pH levels of these shampoos?

WHAT'S THE SCIENCE?

People with curly hair often prefer shampoos with pH levels between 4.5 and 5.5, which are ideal for eliminating static. Flyaway hair is caused by rough hairs rubbing against each other, producing an electrical charge. Some hair-care products use pH adjusters such as citric acid to control flyaway hair by providing a smoothing effect. When hair is at its optimal pH level, which is typically between 4.0 and 5.5, the cuticles lie flat against one another. Closed cuticles have less risk of damage and retain moisture better, keeping hair stronger.

262 FOAM FACTOR

Have you ever wondered why some shampoos are foamier than others?

Materials

- 2 shampoos containing sodium lauryl sulfate (SLS)—check the ingredients list
- 2 shampoos without SLS
- paper and pen
- water

WHAT'S THE SCIENCE?

Sodium lauryl sulfate is a chemical that is found in many shampoos, toothpastes, and mouth rinses. It makes shampoos foamy when lathered. The more sodium lauryl sulfate in a shampoo, the foamier it will be. People with curly hair may prefer products without this chemical. Sulfates strip the hair of the oils that keep curly hair moisturized and shiny.

Steps

1. Make a chart with one row for each shampoo. Note whether it contains sodium lauryl sulfate. Make a column labeled "foam level."
2. Test each shampoo by pouring a little into your hand and mixing in a bit of water. Rub your hands together. Rate the foaminess on a scale of 0–5. Which shampoos are foamier?

263 GO WITH THE FLOW

Get in the know, and go with the flow!

WHAT'S THE SCIENCE?

The term **viscosity** describes a liquid's resistance to flow. Thin liquids tend to have lower viscosity and thick liquids usually have higher viscosity. The shampoos that rolled down the paper and/or dripped are probably highly viscous, while those that stayed in clumps and didn't move are less viscous.

Materials

- a sheet of cardboard
- a sheet of newspaper
- several different kinds of shampoo
- a timer
- a ruler
- pen and paper

Steps

1. Prop the cardboard up against a wall so that it inclines. Lay a sheet of newspaper on the floor, in case of drips.
2. Test each shampoo's viscosity by putting a drop at the top of the cardboard. Use the timer to assess how far it moves in 30 seconds.
3. Measure the distance and calculate how many centimeters or inches per second each shampoo travels by dividing the distance traveled by the time taken (30 seconds).
4. Make a chart with rows listing each of the different shampoos and a column for the distance per second.

264 BREAK IT DOWN

Materials

- saucepan
- ½ cup shampoo
- 5 tablespoons Epsom salts
- spoon

Finally! The perfect solution for those oily hair days!

WHAT'S THE SCIENCE?

At the root of each hair, a sebaceous gland secretes an oily substance called sebum. Oil is less dense than water, and doesn't dissolve in it, so oil isn't removed from hair with water alone. Other substances, known as detergents, can increase the chances that excess oils will be removed from hair by sticking to the oil on one end of its molecule and the water on the other.

Steps

1. Warm the shampoo in the saucepan on the stove—don't let it get too hot.
2. Stir in the Epsom salts.
3. Let the mixture cool.
4. Wash your hair with the Epsom shampoo and then rinse.

265 MOISTURE LOVERS

What's the secret to silky smooth hair?

WHAT'S THE SCIENCE?

Humectants are often added to shampoos to help hair retain moisture. This group of molecules has a special property: they are "water-loving," or **hydrophilic**. This means they are able to "hold" moisture near them— or, in this case, near your skin and hair!

Materials

- 2 shampoos containing humectants (look for Panthenol, which is the most common humectant in shampoos and conditioners)
- 2 shampoos without humectants
- 2 friends
- paper and pen

Steps

1. Make a chart with rows listing each of the different shampoos and a column for the conditioning scores.
2. Ask two friends to use each shampoo for three days in a row. They should rate how moisturized and soft their hair feels after using each shampoo, on a scale of 0–5.
3. Check the scores against the shampoos. Did the shampoos that contain humectants score better?

266 MINTY FRESH

Wake up your face with a minty mask!

WHAT'S THE SCIENCE?

Smells are chemical. As they float in the air, receptors in our noses pick up on them and transmit responses to our brains. Smells can affect our moods—some invigorate while others calm. Peppermint oil contains menthol, which triggers certain receptors in our skin. This causes the "cooling" sensation we experience when menthol is applied.

Materials

- 1 egg
- small bowl
- fork
- 1 teaspoon chopped peppermint leaves
- 1 tablespoon honey
- washcloth

Steps

1. Crack the egg into the bowl and beat it gently with a fork.
2. Stir the peppermint leaves into the egg.
3. Add the honey and mix until you have a paste.
4. Spread the mint mask over your face. Let it dry for 10 minutes.
5. Rinse the mask off using warm water and a washcloth.

267 BAGGAGE BYE-BYE

Fix those bags under your eyes—with teabags!

WHAT'S THE SCIENCE?

Green tea is high in **antioxidants**, which prevent the chemical reactions that damage cells, including skin cells. The antioxidants found in green tea rid your body of toxins and help your cells to function properly.

Materials
- cup
- hot water
- two green teabags

Steps

1. Fill the cup with hot water, then add the teabags and leave them to steep.
2. When the water has cooled, squeeze the teabags gently to remove excess water.
3. Lie down, and place one teabag under each eye.
4. Leave the teabags in place for about 10 minutes. Remove the teabags and enjoy the feeling of relaxed eyes.

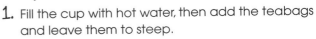

268 SWEET CHEEKS

This simple recipe will leave your skin baby soft and smooth!

WHAT'S THE SCIENCE?

Your skin's outermost layer, the epidermis, contains **keratin**—the same tough protein that can be found in your hair and nails. Raw honey has a protein in it called defensin-1, which acts as an antibacterial agent. Scientists have found its presence helps keep bad bacteria at bay. Yogurt is high in a type of lactic acid called alpha hydroxy, which helps to keep your skin soft and smooth by stimulating the production of collagen and elastin in the skin.

Materials
- 1 tablespoon honey
- bowl
- 1 tablespoon oats
- 1 tablespoon natural yogurt
- spoon
- washcloth

Steps

1. Before placing 1 teaspoon in the bowl, warm the honey by holding the jar in your hands.
2. Add the oats and yogurt and mix them through the honey.
3. Spread the mixture on your face. Leave it on for 15 minutes.
4. Wash your face with warm water and a washcloth.

TEA-RIFFIC!

Treat your hair to this tea-riffic shampoo!

WHAT'S THE SCIENCE?

Without shampoo it can be difficult to wash oil and dirt out of hair, because oil does not mix with water. But shampoo is an **emulsifying agent**. This means it is able to disperse one liquid (oil) into another liquid (water). Shampoo suspends oil and dirt so that it can be removed by water—leaving behind clean hair. In this experiment, the glycerin is the emulsifying agent.

Materials

- 4 tablespoons of herbal tea blossoms, such as chamomile or lavender (available at health-food stores and some pharmacies)
- 1 cup boiling water (careful!)
- coffee filter
- bowl
- liquid soap
- lavender and lemon essential oils
- 1½ tablespoons glycerin (available at most pharmacies)
- funnel
- jar or bottle with a lid

DID YOU KNOW?

Most shampoos also contain some sort of protein that acts as a conditioning agent.

Steps

1. Put the herbal tea blossoms into the boiling water.

2. Stir in the tea blossoms, then leave them to steep for half an hour.

3. Pour the tea through a coffee filter into the bowl. Discard the blossoms.

4. Stir in the liquid soap, then add a few drops each of lavender and lemon oil.

5. Slowly stir in the glycerin, then pour the solution through the funnel and into the jar or bottle.

6. Now treat your hair to some fabulous shampoo!

270 B IS FOR BEAUTY

Give your face some oatmeal for breakfast!

Materials

- ¾ cup dry oatmeal
- ⅓ cup warm water
- washcloth

Steps

1. Mix the oatmeal and warm water until you have formed a paste. You may need to add a little more water.
2. Spread the mask over your face, covering it entirely but keeping the eye area clear.
3. Leave the mask on for 10–15 minutes.
4. Wash off the mask with warm water and a washcloth.

WHAT'S THE SCIENCE?

Oatmeal contains **phenols**, a form of antiseptic. Antiseptics destroy bacteria and other microorganisms. Oatmeal also has anti-inflammatory properties, which is why it is so effective at soothing skin—relieving it of itching and irritation.

271 HONEY BEAR CARE

Treat acne with two simple, natural ingredients!

Materials

- medium-sized apple
- grater
- bowl
- 5 tablespoons raw honey
- washcloth

Steps

1. Grate the apple into a bowl.
2. If the honey is too thick, put it in a small bowl or a glass and hold it, allowing the heat of your hands to melt it a little. Do NOT microwave the honey or heat it on the stove. You will destroy it healing properties—and it can burn!
3. Mix together the apple and honey and pat it onto your skin, focusing on any acne-prone areas.
4. Leave the mask on your face for 10 minutes.
5. Wash your face with warm water and a washcloth.

WHAT'S THE SCIENCE?

Acne can occur when oily sebum is trapped under the skin. The sebum forms a lump and blocks hair tubes, trapping otherwise harmless bacteria that lives on skin. Honey, which has antibacterial properties (especially in its raw state), has been proven to be a successful anti-acne agent for many people.

272

PEARL POLISH

Your smile will be a little brighter after using this homemade toothpaste!

WHAT'S THE SCIENCE?

Baking soda dissolves quickly into water. As it dissolves it loses its abrasive properties, but remains a highly effective detergent. Detergents are effective cleaning agents because they break up oils, which come from food stuck in the teeth.

Materials

- 4 teaspoons baking soda/bicarbonate of soda
- 1 teaspoon almond, peppermint, or vanilla extract
- 1 teaspoon salt
- airtight container

Steps

1. Mix together the baking soda/bicarbonate of soda, extract, and salt.
2. Store the toothpaste in an airtight container between uses.

273

MISS KISS

Your kitchen cupboards have everything you need for soft lips!

WHAT'S THE SCIENCE?

Lip balms contain fatty acids (like the olive oil in this experiment), which moisturize and condition skin. Many lip balms also contain a form of wax, such as beeswax, to seal in moisture. Before it is used in cosmetics, beeswax is often heated in water then mixed with vegetable oil to dilute and soften it.

Materials

- 2 cups water
- saucepan
- grater
- 0.5 oz (14 g) beeswax
- heatproof bowl
- 1 teaspoon honey
- 4 fl oz (120 ml) olive oil
- spoon
- potholders
- small jars with lids

Steps

1. Boil the water in the saucepan on the stove.
2. Grate the beeswax into the heatproof bowl and place it on top of the saucepan (ask an adult for help).
3. Melt the beeswax, then add the honey and olive oil and stir. Don't worry if the honey does not fully mix with the oil.
4. Use potholders to remove the bowl, then set it aside to cool.
5. Spoon the balm into small jars and store for use as necessary.

LIP LICKERS

274

Create your own line of unique lip balms!

WHAT'S THE SCIENCE?

The ingredients in a lip balm affect how it smells, feels, and works. Altering the ingredients you use changes the properties of the lip balm. Some people might prefer their lip balm to be more acidic or more basic, hard or viscous, better moisturizers or more aromatic.

DID YOU KNOW?

If you want a water-resistant lip balm, just make it more viscous!

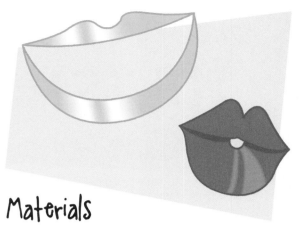

Materials

- saucepan
- water
- heatproof bowl
- 0.5 oz (14 g) beeswax
- grater
- 1 teaspoon honey
- 4 fl oz (120 ml) olive oil
- spoon
- ingredients to adjust the balm's pH level (such as lemon juice or baking soda/bicarbonate of soda)
- water, to adjust the balm's viscosity
- almond oil, peppermint oil, or powdered milk to adjust the balm's moisturizing properties
- peppermint or rose oil to adjust the balm's aroma
- small jars with lids

Steps

1. To make several batches of the lip balm in experiment 273 (Miss Kiss), multiply the ingredients by the number of batches you want to experiment with.

2. Add different ingredients to different lip balm batches. What can you add to make your formula more acidic or basic? Lemon juice? Baking soda/bicarbonate of soda? How would any of these affect the consistency of your balm?

3. Play around with the viscosity of your formula. More beeswax will make the balm harder, while more water will make it thinner and more viscous.

4. Try making your balm a super moisturizer. One or more fatty acids (such as the almond oil, peppermint oil or powdered milk) might do the trick.

5. Which essential oils provide the most pleasing aromas?

275 THE PERFUME LAB

Can't find a perfume you like? Make your own!

WHAT'S THE SCIENCE?

When perfume is applied to skin, the fragrance is released as body heat rises. Perfumes smell different on different people because of differences in body chemistry. A perfume will usually smell stronger and last longer on a person with oily skin, and will fade more quickly on a person with dry skin.

Materials

- bottle
- 0.5 fl oz (15 ml) almond oil
- base note scents: cinnamon, clove, ginger, jasmine, or sandalwood essential oils (use one or more)
- middle note scents: fennel, geranium, lavender, nutmeg, or rosemary essential oils (use one or more)
- top note scents: basil, grapefruit, lemon, lime, rose, or peppermint (use one or more)

WARNING: Those with nut allergies may be sensitive to this experiment as it uses almond oil!

Steps

1. Pour the almond oil into your bottle.
2. Add seven "base note" drops.
3. Add seven "middle note" drops.
4. Add seven "top note" drops.
5. Shake the bottle to combine the oils, then dab a bit of your new perfume on each wris

276 AIR CARE

Just as sound travels, so do scents!

WHAT'S THE SCIENCE?

Water can be a liquid, a solid (such as ice), and a vapor (a gas). Water can also be "atomized." When a liquid is atomized, it is dispersed into air. A perfect example of atomized liquid is sprayed perfume. The scent is molecules that evaporate from the source of the smell and bounce off other molecules in the air. Once sprayed, the smell disperses; as the molecules bounce, they diffuse and become equally spread out in the room. Air temperature affects how fast the molecules move: the warmer the room, the faster the molecules disperse.

Materials

- perfume in spray bottle
- 4 chairs
- 4 friends/family members
- timer

Steps

1. Arrange four chairs one behind the other, leading from the front of the room to the back.
2. Ask each person to sit in a chair.
3. Stand at the front of the room and spray some perfume into the air.
4. Ask each person to raise their hand when they smell the perfume. Time how long it takes before each hand is raised.

277 PERFUME PILLOW

Could lavender help you sleep better? Give it a try!

WHAT'S THE SCIENCE?

Lavender contains a chemical called linalool. More than 200 plant species produce linalool. It is used in detergents, lotions, mosquito repellents, shampoos, and soaps because of its strong scent. Many people believe that linalool has calming properties.

Materials

- handkerchief
- dried lavender (and other herbs such as chamomile if you have them handy)
- cinnamon sticks, broken into pieces
- ribbon

Steps

1. Lay the handkerchief flat on a table.
2. Fill the center with a few tablespoons of lavender and other dried herbs, if using.
3. Add some broken cinnamon sticks to the mixture.
4. Pull the corners of the handkerchief together and tie the bag closed with a ribbon. Tuck your new sachet into your pillow.

278 YOU WITH A HUE

Have some body paint fun— and get picture-perfect skin!

WHAT'S THE SCIENCE?

Cornstarch is a "binder" that is used as a thickener in many foods, including puddings, gravy, and soup. Cornstarch thickens by having the free starch molecules swell; when they swell, they absorb moisture. Cornstarch also absorbs oils, which is why many cosmetic manufacturers use it in products designed to control oily skin.

Materials

- 1 teaspoon cornstarch/ cornflour
- ½ teaspoon cold cream
- small bowl
- ½ teaspoon water
- food coloring (be careful when using food coloring, as it will stain)
- spoon
- small glass j[e] with airtight
- paintbrush

Steps

1. Mix the cornstarch/cornflour and cold cream together in the small bowl. Add the water and st[ir]
2. Add the food coloring one drop at a time until you are happy with the color. Stir well after each drop has been added.
3. Spoon the body paint into the jar. Grab your paintbrush and get started! The body paint will wash off with warm water.

279 SOLID SCENTS

You won't have to worry about spilling THIS perfume!

Materials

- 2 cups water
- saucepan
- 1 tablespoon beeswax
- grater
- heatproof bowl
- long wooden stirring stick
- 1 tablespoon almond oil
- 10 drops of essential oils such as jasmine or rose
- small bowl or container

WARNING: Those with nut allergies may be sensitive to this experiment as it uses almond oil!

WHAT'S THE SCIENCE?

All matter exists in one of three states: liquid, gas, or solid. The atoms in solids are close together and move very slowly. In gases, the atoms are far apart, and bounce off each other quickly. Liquids are in between. Most perfumes are liquid, but some perfumes do come in solid form—as proven in this experiment!

DID YOU KNOW?

In Japan, people sometimes put a dab of solid perfume on their business cards!

Steps

1. Place the water in the saucepan and boil on the stove.
2. Grate the beeswax into the heatproof bowl, then place it on top of the saucepan (ask an adult for help).
3. Stir the beeswax until it is completely liquid, then stir in the almond oil and essential oils.
4. Use potholders to remove the bowl from the saucepan.
5. Pour the liquid wax into a small bowl or container. Leave it to cool and harden for half an hour.
6. To apply your solid perfume, rub a finger on its surface then dab it on your wrist or neck!

She did it!

Elizabeth Arden
Canada

Elizabeth Arden was born in 1884 in Canada. She studied nursing for a while, but dropped out to join her older brother in New York City. There, she worked as a bookkeeper for a pharmaceutical company. Her job meant she spent many hours in laboratories, where she gained a deeper understanding of the essentials of skin care. Elizabeth traveled to France, where she studied in salons, mastering beauty techniques. She began experimenting with her own formulas for lipsticks, rouges, and powders. Elizabeth opened her first beauty salon in 1910, and soon had salons all over the world. Her cosmetic brand has been an industry leader since 1930!

280 GLITTER GEL

Spread this gel on your arms and legs to give yourself an extra-sparkly appearance!

WHAT'S THE SCIENCE?

Many beauty products list water as one of their main ingredients. The aloe vera in this recipe is a perfect water substitute. It has a water content of nearly 96%, but also contains vitamins, **enzymes**, sugars, minerals, **saponins**, **lignin**, **salicylic acid**, and **amino acids**. The aloe vera plant has thick leaves and grows in arid areas including Africa, India, Nepal, and North America.

Materials

- ½ cup aloe vera gel (clear is best)
- 1 teaspoon glycerin (available at most pharmacies)
- small bowl
- 2 teaspoons glitter (whatever color you're in the mood for!)
- spoon
- small glass jar with airtight lid

Steps

1. Mix the gel and glycerin together in the small bowl.
2. Sprinkle in the glitter and stir well.
3. Spoon the mixture into the small glass jar.
4. Spread some gel on whenever you need to add some sparkle to your day!

281 SHIMMER POWDER

Polish your perfect skin with a pearlescent shimmer!

Materials

- 4 tablespoons cornstarch/cornflour
- 1 teaspoon glitter
- small bowl
- spoon
- small glass jar with airtight lid

WHAT'S THE SCIENCE?

Objects that are **pearlescent** have a pearly, silvery finish. Pearlescent pigments are used to color face, eye, lip, and nail makeup. Chemists create pearlescent substances through special **crystallization** processes using mica, iron oxide, and titanium oxide.

Steps

1. Combine the cornstarch/cornflour and glitter in a small bowl and stir together.
2. Spoon the powder into a small glass jar. Rub some onto your skin when you want to shimmer and shine!

282 VITA-MAZING

Know which juice to pick when you need a quick dose of Vitamin C?

WHAT'S THE SCIENCE?

Vitamin C, which contributes to healthy skin, is found in many fruit juices. Oranges are particularly high in vitamin C. The indicator you will make in this experiment is similar to an acid-base indicator but instead, it will change color when vitamin C is present. Don't be fooled—some "orange drinks" are not as good for you as you might think!

Materials

- 1 cup cold water
- saucepan
- 1 teaspoon cornstarch/cornflour
- large container
- eye dropper
- 1 gal (4 L) water
- 1 teaspoon iodine
- several jars
- fruit juices, such as orange and apple, and orange drinks (such as orange soda/soft drink)

DID YOU KNOW?

Foods that are particularly high in vitamin C include broccoli, green peppers/capsicums, oranges, strawberries, and tomatoes!

Steps

1. Pour the cold water into the saucepan, then stir in the cornstarch/cornflour.

2. Heat the water on the stove until it is boiling (ask an adult for help), then let it sit for two minutes.

3. In a large container, combine 1 gal (4 L) water with 10 eye droppers of the cornstarch liquid. Add one eye dropper of iodine and stir. This solution is your "indicator."

4. Fill each jar about 0.25 in (0.5 cm) high with the indicator solution.

5. Place one drop of orange juice in the first jar. Continue adding juice, one drop at a time. How quickly does the indicator change color?

6. In the second jar, repeat with apple juice.

7. Continue to test different juices and drinks. The juices that contain the most vitamin C will change the indicator's color the quickest!

283 YUMMY YOGURT

Make your own yogurt and enjoy the health and beauty benefits!

WHAT'S THE SCIENCE?

Your body needs a certain amount of "good bacteria" to help with digestion. Yogurts contain these good bacteria, which are also called "probiotics." As yogurt is made, bacteria affect the sugars (lactose) in the milk—lowering its pH and making it more acidic. The bacteria also make yogurt last longer.

Materials

- 1 qt (950 ml) whole milk
- saucepan
- instant-read thermometer
- large bowl
- cold water
- 1 tablespoon plain yogurt with active cultures
- large jar
- cooler/esky
- small bucket of hot water

Steps

1. Heat the milk in the saucepan on the stove (ask an adult for help). Bring it to 195° F (90° C)—just below boiling point.
2. Reduce the heat and leave the milk on the stove for 10 minutes.
3. Fill a large bowl with cold water.
4. Remove the saucepan from the stove and place it in the cold water. Wait until the temperature is about 110° F (43° C), then stir in the yogurt.
5. Transfer the mixture into the jar and place it in the cooler/esky. Put the bucket of hot water in the cooler as well. Leave the yogurt for 24 hours.

284 PINEAPPLE SURPRISE

A diet rich in fruits is vital for healthy skin and hair!

WHAT'S THE SCIENCE?

If pineapple is mixed into gelatin, the gelatin will melt. Gelatin becomes solid when proteins bond together and hold the solution in a semi-solid state. Enzymes from the pineapple cut the bonds between the proteins, causing the gelatin to return to its liquid state.

Materials

- box of gelatin
- 2 containers
- ½ cup ripe pineapple or tinned pineapple chunks
- knife (ask an adult for help)

Steps

1. Prepare the gelatin according to the instructions on the box.
2. Pour half of the finished solution into one container and the other half into the second container. Leave to cool.
3. Cut the pineapple into chunks.
4. Put a handful of pineapple chunks into one of the containers.
5. Wait for several hours. Do both lots of gelatin set?

★ 285 BEAT IT!

Who says getting your daily dose of protein can't be SWEET!

WHAT'S THE SCIENCE?

Eggs are high in protein, which is essential for good health. The healthier you are inside, the healthier you will appear on the outside! Proteins are shaped by hydrogen bonds that make them curl up and twist. When you beat the egg whites to make meringue, some of the hydrogen bonds in the protein break. This causes the protein's structure to unfold. It is this change in structure that leads to a meringue's stiff consistency.

DID YOU KNOW?

Egg whites and sugar are both **hygroscopic** *(water-attracting) chemicals. This is why meringue becomes soggy when refrigerated or stored in a high-humidity environment. It is also why you sometimes see meringue "weep" or "sweat" with beads of moisture on its surface.*

Materials

- baking tray
- wax paper
- 3 egg whites
- pinch of salt
- electric mixer with whisk attachment
- 6 oz (170 g) berry/caster sugar
- large spoon

Steps

1. Preheat your oven to 300° F (150° C).
2. Line the baking tray with wax paper.
3. Whisk the egg whites and salt. Start the mixer on low for about a minute, then increase the speed to medium until the egg whites form stiff peaks.
4. Increase the speed to fast, then add the sugar a little at a time until the mixture is glossy and stiff.
5. Spoon large dollops of meringue onto the tray, leaving a space between each one.
6. Bake the meringues for half an hour. Leave them in longer if necessary. They are "done" when they appear dry and pale.
7. Turn off the oven but leave the meringues inside until they have cooled.

286 BERRYLICIOUS SMOOTHIE

Try this smoothie to add some flavor to your day!

Materials

- 1 large banana
- 1 cup fresh blueberries
- ½ cup low-fat yogurt (vanilla is best)
- 1 cup low-fat milk
- ¾ cup crushed ice
- blender or food processor
- large glass

Steps

1. Put all of the ingredients into the blender or food processor. Mix well (ask an adult for help).
2. Pour into a large glass and enjoy!
3. Enjoy this smoothie several mornings a week. Do you notice a difference in how you feel after a month? Do your hair and skin look and feel healthier?

WHAT'S THE SCIENCE?

Fruits and vegetables are colored by natural plant pigments. The plant pigments that give red and blue/purple fruits and vegetables are lycopene and anthocyanins. These protect your body's cells from damage. The plant pigments that color orange fruits and vegetables are carotenoids. Studies have proven that these are good for your heart. Green fruits and vegetables are colored by chlorophyll which strengthens your immune system.

287 GREEN QUEEN

This super smoothie will transform you into a green goddess!

Materials

- 1 cherry tomato
- 1 chopped celery stalk
- 1 cucumber
- 3 leaves of spinach
- 1 cup yogurt
- 6 ice cubes
- blender
- large glass

Steps

1. Put all of the ingredients into the blender. Mix well (ask an adult for help).
2. Pour into a large glass and enjoy!
3. Enjoy this smoothie a few times a week for several weeks. What do you notice about the way you look and feel after making it part of your regular diet?

WHAT'S THE SCIENCE?

Getting enough of the right vitamins and minerals is important for your body's health—especially if you're still growing! Many green vegetables (such as beans and broccoli) are high in magnesium, which is important for bones and muscles. Leafy greens (such as spinach) are often high in iron, which helps your body form healthy red blood cells. The more colorful the vegetable, the more nutrient-rich it is likely to be.

WONDER WORDS

acidic—Having an excess of hydrogen atoms; a pH less than 7.

alkaline—A basic substance.

amino acids—Organic acids that are the building blocks of proteins.

anode—The negative terminal of a battery.

antacid—A neutralizing agent that counteracts acidity.

antioxidants—Substances that protect the body's cells from oxidation damage.

atoms—The building blocks of all matter. An atom is the smallest particle of a substance that still has the properties of that substance. The various types of atoms are called elements. An atom of gold, for example, is the smallest particle of that element possible.

basic—Having a low concentration of hydrogen ions; a pH greater than 7.

cathode—The positive terminal of a battery.

cellular—To do with or consisting of cells.

compound—A substance made of two or more chemical elements bonded together.

crystallization—The process of something forming crystals.

electrons—The smallest of three particles that make up atoms (sub-atomic particles). These carry a negative charge and surround the nucleus of an atom.

emollients—Substances that soften and soothe skin.

emulsifying agent—A substance that blends two or more liquids, such as oil and water, that would otherwise repel one another.

enzymes—Proteins that are capable of producing chemical change in organic substances.

evaporate—To convert into a gas.

humectant—A substance that helps another substance retain moisture.

hydrogen ion—Positively charged particles, or protons, formed when hydrogen loses electrons.

hydrophylic—Having a strong affinity for water.

hygroscopic—Able to absorb or attract moisture from the air.

ion—An atom or molecule with a positive or negative electric charge due to the loss or gain of one or more electrons.

keratin—A protein found in the outer layer of feathers, hair, hooves, nails, and skin.

leavening agent—Agents that help to lighten the texture and increase the volume of baked goods by producing CO_2 (carbon dioxide).

lignin—A substance found in wood, which is similar to the cell wall. It adds rigidity to the wood the tree form.

molecules—Molecules are several atoms bonded together.

neutralized—Made neutral by combining equal acidic and basic components.

pearlescent—Having a pearly, iridescent luster.

phenols—An acidic compound found in coal and wood, and used as a disinfectant.

pH levels—Measurements indicating how acidic or basic a solution is, ranging from 0–14, with 7 as neutral. pH stands for potential Hydrogen.

polymers—Chemical compounds formed from long chains of the same molecule group, with high boiling and melting points.

properties—The qualities or characteristics of matter or of a substance.

salicylic acid—A substance that counters bacteria and fungi, used as a food preservative and an antiseptic.

saponification—A process that turns fat into soap.

saponins—Plant glycosides that form emulsions and foam when mixed with water; for example, detergents.

solvent—A solid, liquid or gas in which another solid, liquid or gas is dissolved.

triglycerides—A type of fat molecule. They are the main molecule in oils, such as vegetable oil.

viscosity—The resistance of a fluid to flow; a measurement of a liquid's "thickness."

Text © Kirsten Hall 2012, 2014

Experiments adapted from *365 Science Experiments* (originally published as *501 Science Experiments*) remain © Hinkler Books Pty Ltd
Design/illustration/book title © Hinkler Books Pty Ltd 2012, 2014

Author: Kirsten Hall

Science consultant: Kim Chaloner B.S., M.A.

Internal design and layout: Tim Palin Creative

Illustrations: Charlie Alder

Cover design: Ginny Westcott